500 RECIPES FOR CHICKEN DISHES

by Marguerite Patten

HAMLYN
LONDON · NEW YORK · SYDNEY · TORONTO

Published by The Hamlyn Publishing Group Limited
London · New York · Sydney · Toronto
Astronaut House, Feltham, Middlesex, England

Printed in England by Cox & Wyman Ltd.,
London, Reading and Fakenham

Contents

Introduction

Once chicken was regarded as a luxury but nowadays, due to extensive and carefully planned breeding, this poultry has become one of the more economical protein foods. Chicken is easily digested so is suitable for all members of the family; it is also very versatile. Larger birds can be roasted, boiled or braised with stuffings and interesting sauces to accompany them. Jointed young chickens are suitable for frying or grilling in various ways and provide a nourishing meal in a matter of minutes

Sometimes frozen chickens can be cheaper than fresh birds; these are very satisfactory if you follow the advice given in the first chapter.

Thrifty housewives will appreciate the fact that even the chicken carcass can be used, to provide a well flavoured stock for soups, sauces and stews. I have also included a section of special occasion recipes using chicken in order to illustrate its suitability for gourmet as well as family dishes.

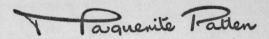

Useful facts and figures

Notes on metrication

In this book quantities are given in metric and Imperial measures. Exact conversion from Imperial to metric measures does not usually give very convenient working quantities and so the metric measures have been rounded off into units of 25 grams. The table below shows the recommended equivalents.

Ounces	Approx g to nearest whole figure	Recommended conversion to nearest unit of 25
1	28	25
2	57	50
3	85	75
4	113	100
5	142	150
6	170	175
7	198	200
8	227	225
9	255	250
10	283	275
11	312	300
12	340	350
13	368	375
14	396	400
15	425	425
16 (1 lb)	454	450
17	482	475
18	510	500
19	539	550
20 (1¼ lb)	567	575

Note:
When converting quantities over 20 oz first add the appropriate figures in the centre column, then adjust to the nearest unit of 25. As a general guide, 1 kg (1000 g) equals 2·2 lb or about 2 lb 3 oz. This method of conversion gives good results in nearly all cases, although in certain pastry and cake recipes a more accurate conversion is necessary to produce a balanced recipe.

Liquid measures: The millilitre has been used in this book and the following table gives a few examples.

Imperial	Approx ml to nearest whole figure	Recommended ml
¼ pint	142	150 ml
½ pint	283	300 ml
¾ pint	425	450 ml
1 pint	567	600 ml
1½ pints	851	900 ml
1¾ pints	992	1000 ml (1 litre)

Spoon measures: All spoon measures given in this book are level unless otherwise stated.

Can sizes: At present, cans are marked with the exact (usually to the nearest whole number) metric equivalent of the Imperial weight of the contents, so we have followed this practice when giving can sizes.

Oven temperatures

The table below gives recommended equivalents.

	°C	°F	Gas Mark
Very cool	110	225	$\frac{1}{4}$
	120	250	$\frac{1}{2}$
Cool	140	275	1
	150	300	2
Moderate	160	325	3
	180	350	4
Moderately hot	190	375	5
	200	400	6
Hot	220	425	7
	230	450	8
Very hot	240	475	9

Notes for American and Australian users

In America the 8-oz measuring cup is used. In Australia metric measures are now used in conjunction with the standard 250-ml measuring cup. The Imperial pint, used in Britain and Australia, is 20 fl oz, while the American pint is 16 fl oz. It is important to remember that the Australian tablespoon differs from both the British and American tablespoons; the table below gives a comparison. The British standard tablespoon, which has been used throughout this book, holds 17·7 ml, the American 14·2 ml, and the Australian 20 ml. A teaspoon holds approximately 5 ml in all three countries.

British	American	Australian
1 teaspoon	1 teaspoon	1 teaspoon
1 tablespoon	1 tablespoon	1 tablespoon
2 tablespoons	3 tablespoons	2 tablespoons
$3\frac{1}{2}$ tablespoons	4 tablespoons	3 tablespoons
4 tablespoons	5 tablespoons	$3\frac{1}{2}$ tablespoons

An Imperial-American guide to solid and liquid measures

Solid measures

IMPERIAL	AMERICAN
1 lb butter or margarine	2 cups
1 lb flour	4 cups
1 lb granulated or castor sugar	2 cups
1 lb icing sugar	3 cups
8 oz rice	1 cup

Liquid measures

IMPERIAL	AMERICAN
$\frac{1}{4}$ pint liquid	$\frac{2}{3}$ cup liquid
$\frac{1}{2}$ pint	$1\frac{1}{4}$ cups
$\frac{3}{4}$ pint	2 cups
1 pint	$2\frac{1}{2}$ cups
$1\frac{1}{2}$ pints	$3\frac{3}{4}$ cups
2 pints	5 cups ($2\frac{1}{2}$ pints)

Note:
When making any of the recipes in this book, only follow one set of measures as they are not interchangeable.

Buying and Preparing Chicken

Choosing fresh poultry

While quite a high standard of poultry is usually available, you can get the very best produce if you take extra care in choosing. The flesh of fresh chickens should never have an unpleasant smell.

Capon is the term used to describe large young cockerels that have been castrated and fattened. This gives particularly tender flesh and plump 'meaty' birds suitable for roasting.

Fowl is a term often used to describe an older bird which, while not suitable for roasting or other quick methods of cooking, is excellent when cooked slowly by boiling.

Spring chicken or *poussin* or *broiler* all describe a very young bird, specially bred to be cooked by frying, grilling or other speedy methods. A poussin generally weighs only 500–600 g/1–1¼ lb, whereas the other young chickens can weigh up to 1–1·25 kg/2–2½ lb.

When buying fresh roasting chickens or capons
1 The flesh should look white and firm.
2 The wishbone should feel soft and pliable.
3 The legs should be bright yellow and fresh-looking with firm claws.
4 In the case of a cock the comb should be firm and bright in colour.
5 The breast should be broad, which means you can carve generous slices from this.
6 Do *not* buy a chicken which has little breast and very long legs (or you will pay for the weight of bone and not flesh).

When buying fresh boiling fowls
1 The skin of a boiling fowl should have a slightly yellow tinge, which indicates a certain amount of fat.
2 Do *not* buy a boiling fowl, however, if the layer of fat is very thick (or the fat will run out during cooking and leave you with relatively little meat).
3 Signs of freshness are the same as for roasting chicken.

When buying fresh spring chickens
1 There should be a reasonable amount of flesh on the breast (otherwise you are buying skin and bone).
2 Signs of freshness are the same as for roasting chicken.

When buying fresh jointed chickens
1 Where possible choose the same sort of joints – all legs, all breasts – for a particular dish.

2 The legs should be well covered with flesh, which should not be too dark (or it could indicate staleness).
3 All other points are similar to those for whole chickens.

Quantities of poultry to allow

1 Really large chickens or capons should give 6–9 portions and should be carved in slices (see page 8).
2 A smaller chicken gives 4–5 portions. You can either carve in slices or divide the bird into 2 wing/breast portions and 2 leg portions.
3 A really small spring chicken provides a generous portion for one, but a slightly larger bird will serve 2.
4 Naturally the number of portions will also depend upon the accompaniments and other ingredients used.

Preparing poultry

It must be remembered that poultry is handled in the shop, particularly if it has been trussed and jointed, and it should, therefore, be washed well both outside and inside the body. If roasting or frying, dry thoroughly with soft absorbent paper to prevent unnecessary spitting when the bird goes into the fat. Always *remove giblets* from the bird before cooking. These can then be used to make soups, stuffings etc. (see pages 13, 38, 44 and 45). For information on using *frozen* poultry see page 8; information on *freezing* prepared and cooked dishes is given at the beginning of each chapter.

Most chickens sold today are already drawn and trussed, but at some point it may be necessary for you to do it. Most shops will joint a chicken if you ask them to, but you may wish to deal with the matter yourself. Boning may sound an extremely difficult operation, but it can be done by an amateur with patience and it does produce a chicken that can be economically used for party dishes providing a generous number of portions. It also saves any difficulties in carving, since you slice across the bird. Once again, given reasonable notice, a butcher would probably do this for you. Instructions follow for all these operations.

To draw a chicken

1 Cut off the feet and if necessary draw the sinews from the legs by pulling firmly.
2 Hold the bird by the legs and singe to remove any hairs.
3 Cut off the head, leaving about 7·5 cm/3 inches of neck at this stage.
4 Insert a small pointed knife at the top end of the spine and split up the skin of the neck.
5 Pull away loose skin and cut off the neck close to the shoulder, but leave a little of the skin that covered the neck in case you want to stuff both ends of the bird.
6 Remove the crop and windpipe.
7 Cut round the vent, leaving plenty of skin to form a covering round a stuffing. Insert fingers and loosen the organs inside, being careful not to break the gall bladder (attached to the liver) – this would make the flesh so bitter it would be inedible.
8 Firmly draw out all the inside organs, and cut the gall bladder from the liver.
9 Put the neck, liver, gizzard, heart and kidneys into a bowl of cold water and wash thoroughly. Simmer these gently in fresh water to make stock or gravy. Discard the gall bladder.
10 Wipe the inside of the bird with a clean damp cloth.

To truss a chicken

A chicken is trussed so that it will keep its shape while cooking. Stuff the chicken before trussing.

1 Insert the stuffing at the breast end. If two kinds of stuffing are used, one kind can be put in at the other end.
2 Fold the skin firmly over the back at the neck end.
3 Press the legs down firmly on to the thighs at the sides of the bird.
4 Put a poultry skewer right through the bird where the thighs meet the legs.
5 Turn the bird over and pinion the wings to the loose skin of the neck with another skewer.
6 Pass soft uncoloured string under the ends of the first skewer and cross it over the breast.
7 Turn the bird over, slide the crossed string towards the tail and tie the string round it, securing the ends of the legs.

To joint a chicken – Method 1

1 Insert a large sharp knife to one side of the breast-bone and cut the chicken in half along the bone.
2 Then cut through the skin between each leg and the body to uncover the joint; pull back the leg. Cut through the joint.
3 To divide each leg into 2 pieces, cut through the joint between the drumstick and the thigh bone.
4 Lift each wing and cut through the skin between the wing and the breast to uncover the joint. Cut along the breast and through the joint, leaving some breast meat on the wing portion.
5 The back of the bird has very little meat, but the bones can be used with the giblets and neck for stocks.

To joint a chicken – Method 2 (French style)

This method of jointing a chicken produces a larger number of joints.

1 Cut off the legs by pulling each one gently away from the bird and cutting through the joint. Cut each leg into 2 pieces by cutting through the joint between the drumstick and the thigh bone.
2 Cut off the wings by lifting each one and cutting through the skin between the wing and the breast to uncover the joint. Trim the ends of the wings and drumsticks.
3 Cut the body in half lengthwise along the breastbone.
4 Cut each piece of breast diagonally across into 2 pieces. Tap the knife gently with a heavy weight if necessary to cut through the bone.
5 Cut the back (undercarriage) into 3 pieces. They can be cooked and used to build up the centre of the dish when serving. (They would not normally be served as portions, but flesh from the back can be used in dishes where small chicken pieces are required.)

To bone and stuff a chicken

1 Commence at the breast with the neck towards you. Loosen the skin at the neck of the bird. (This is easier to do with the tips of your fingers than with a knife.) Continue loosening the skin of the breast away from the flesh, but do not tear the skin.
2 Carefully cut the wishbone away from the flesh with a very sharp small knife so that no meat is left on the bone. Remove the wishbone.
3 Place the bird on its breast and, using the point of the knife, first cut the shoulder joints (by the neck) then cut away the shoulder bones and remove them.
4 Put the tip of the knife into the skin of the wings and neatly cut away the bones from the wings (the tips are better removed completely).
5 Lift skin away from the thighs. Cut the thigh joint away from the body, then gradually cut the flesh away from both thigh bones and drumsticks. (You can leave the small pieces of bone at the base of the drumsticks which join the drumstick to the foot of the bird as this helps to re-form the bird into its familiar shape.)
6 Having removed the wishbone, shoulder bone, wings and legs, you now work carefully to remove the meat from the complete breastbone and backbone. Finally cut off the tail (by the vent). The action here must be slow and careful, scraping and pushing to ease the flesh away from the bones with the help of the knife. The bird can now be flattened.
7 Put the stuffing (you will need at least twice the usual amount) first on to the breast of the boned bird, then put a little down the centre of the leg and wing flesh.
8 Fold the skin at the neck end very firmly over the stuffing to keep it from falling out during cooking.
9 Press the flesh over the stuffing in the legs and wings.
10 Form the flesh and stuffing back into the shape of

the unboned bird (this is not difficult to do as the flesh is soft and pliable).

11 Tie legs and wings firmly into position, arranging the bones at the end of the legs against the body of the bird.

12 Cook in the usual way, allowing just over the normal cooking time for the weight of the bird and stuffing, since this is now solid flesh without bones to conduct the heat. To carve, cut slices right across the bird, so each portion will have light meat, stuffing and dark meat. The bones make excellent stock.

To carve a chicken

The method used depends on the size of the bird. For tiny spring chickens serve 1 per person, or if slightly larger, cut into halves: cut firmly down, slightly to one side of the centre of the breastbone.

Medium chickens can be jointed, rather than carved, making one or two joints of each of the legs and two joints of the breast and wings. For children, each breast and wing could be divided into two portions. The large chicken or capon is carved by first cutting or pulling off the leg on one side. This enables large slices to be cut from the breast. When sufficient meat from the breast has been cut, carve the meat from the leg. Repeat on the other side.

Frozen poultry

Never cook whole poultry when frozen, and do not defrost by immersing it in hot water. Allow the chicken to thaw out gradually. This is best done by leaving the bird in its transparent pack to thaw naturally in the refrigerator. A medium bird will take about 12 hours, but a large capon can take 24 hours at least. In an emergency chickens may be thawed more rapidly by submerging in cold water for 2–3 hours. Leave the birds in their transparent packs and change the water frequently. It is often possible to cook frozen chicken portions without defrosting; the individual recipes will give more information on this point. All the recipes in this book are equally suitable for frozen and fresh chicken.

If you freeze a fresh chicken it keeps for a total of 12 months, but if you freeze fat boiling chickens it is wise to use these within a shorter period, i.e. 6–8 months, as after a longer period the fat may become rancid. Always pack the giblets in a separate container, as these should be used within 3 months.

Using all parts of the chicken

The chicken flesh can be eaten hot or cold in literally hundreds of recipes as shown in this book.

The giblets, i.e. the neck, stomach, kidneys, heart and liver, provide the basis for stocks, soups and other recipes. Never use the gall bladder.

The carcass can be used to make excellent stock (use any chicken skin as well to give extra flavour).

The chicken fat mentioned in many recipes is obtained from simmering a boiling fowl or carcass and skimming the top of the cold stock, or after roasting chicken.

To use canned chicken

Since canned chicken is already cooked, it can be used in recipes which call for the chicken to be reheated, or it can be coated with egg and crumbs and fried or grilled. Be careful not to overcook.

To use turkey

Although this book has been written to give you ideas for using chicken, turkey meat can be substituted in many of the recipes. Turkey portions are frequently available, which are ideal for a small family. Treat these like chicken, but remember that as turkey tends to be drier in texture than chicken you must be generous with the fat in cooking it.

Starters and soups

Hors d'oeuvre and appetisers

Chicken meat, including the giblets, can be used to make interesting hors d'oeuvre. Several of these recipes can also be used for cocktail savouries.
Chicken balls can be frozen for a period of 2 months, but the pâté, rillette and terrine are better if used within 4–6 weeks. Allow these to defrost at room temperature or in the refrigerator. The other dishes should be freshly prepared, although defrosted cooked chicken could be used as an ingredient.

Chicken balls

you will need for 24–36 balls:

METRIC/IMPERIAL

225 g/8 oz raw chicken breast	2 teaspoons cornflour
40 g/1½ oz butter	I egg or 2 egg yolks
salt and pepper	few drops double cream

1 Finely mince the chicken meat and blend with the rest of the ingredients.
2 Form into small balls using a damp teaspoon.
3 Poach in steadily boiling salted water for 8 minutes; do not allow the water to boil too rapidly.
4 Serve on soups, or cool and coat with mayonnaise then arrange on a bed of salad.

Variations:
Almond chicken balls: Prepare chicken balls to stage 3. Brush with lightly whisked egg white and roll in very finely chopped almonds. Deep fry for 3–4 minutes; drain on absorbent paper and serve hot or cold.

Curried chicken balls: Add 1 teaspoon curry paste and 2 teaspoons smooth chutney at stage 1 and omit the cream. Poach as stage 3.

Parmesan chicken balls: Prepare and cook the chicken balls to stage 4, cool then roll in finely grated Parmesan cheese and chopped parsley.

Soufflé balls: Prepare and cook the chicken balls to stage 4. Meanwhile blend 50 g/2 oz flour with 2 egg yolks, 5 tablespoons water and 2 stiffly whisked egg whites. Coat the warm chicken balls with this mixture and deep fry for 2 minutes; serve hot as an appetiser.

Speedy chicken mousse

serves 3–4

Blend 225 g/8 oz finely minced cooked chicken with 150 ml/¼ pint whipped cream, 1–2 tablespoons thick mayonnaise (see page 80), seasoning, a few drops of Worcestershire or Tabasco sauce and/or sherry. Spoon on to crisp lettuce.

Chicken liver pâté

Chicken livers make an excellent pâté; often you can buy them frozen.

you will need for 4–6 servings:

METRIC/IMPERIAL

350 g/12 oz chicken livers	4 tablespoons chicken stock or single cream
I onion	salt and pepper
I clove garlic (optional)	
50 g/2 oz butter or chicken fat	

1 Wash, dry and halve the livers; peel and grate or chop the onion and garlic.
2 Heat the butter or fat in a pan and fry the livers with the onion and garlic for 5–6 minutes, taking care they do not discolour.
3 Add the stock or cream and seasoning; heat for 1–2 minutes more then chop, sieve or liquidise the mixture and allow to cool in a dish. Top with melted butter to prevent it drying out.
4 Serve with lemon wedges, lettuce and crisp hot toast and butter.

Note:
A little sherry or brandy can be substituted for some of the stock or cream.

Variations:
Chicken pâté: Add 175 g/6 oz cooked minced or sieved chicken breast at stage 3 for a milder pâté. You will need an extra 1–2 tablespoons stock or other liquid to compensate for the extra dry ingredient.

Liver and tongue pâté: Add 175 g/6 oz cooked tongue at stage 3 as well as an extra 1–2 tablespoons stock.

Aspic moulds

serves 4–6

Dice 225 g/8 oz cooked chicken breast. Make up 600 ml/1 pint aspic jelly with water or chicken stock and allow to cool. Blend the chicken, some cooked peas and 2 chopped hard-boiled eggs into the jelly. Spoon into small oiled moulds and leave to set. Serve with salad.

Chopped liver

you will need for 4 servings:

METRIC/IMPERIAL

225 g/8 oz chicken livers	40 g/1½ oz chicken fat
1 medium onion	salt and pepper
2 eggs	

1 Wash the livers and dry thoroughly on absorbent paper; peel and chop the onion.
2 Hard-boil the eggs, then shell and chop them.
3 Heat the chicken fat and fry the livers and onion in it until soft; finely chop the livers and season well.
4 Top with the chopped egg and serve with thin toast and butter.

Variations:

Potted liver: At stage 4 mince or liquidise the seasoned liver.

Potted chicken: Cook tender diced raw chicken in a generous amount of butter, add salt, pepper and grated nutmeg, and mince, chop or liquidise. Serve potted meats with toast or in sandwiches.

Rillette of chicken

serves 2–3

This is an economical and interesting way to use chicken giblets. Simmer the giblets until tender in water to cover, with seasoning to taste. Meanwhile fry a peeled chopped onion in 50 g/2 oz butter (a crushed clove of garlic can be added if liked). Chop the giblets, removing all meat from the neck, then pound or liquidise with the onion, any butter remaining in the pan and enough stock or single cream to make a soft consistency. Serve with hot toast and butter in place of pâté. The giblets may be flavoured with a little chopped rosemary or thyme, diced gherkin or sherry.

Chicken terrine (Pâté de Bruxelles)

you will need for 6–8 servings:

METRIC/IMPERIAL

2–2.25-kg/4½–5-lb roasting chicken with giblets	100 ml/4 fl oz sherry or brandy
450 g/1 lb pork or veal	1 egg
salt and pepper	450 g/1 lb fatty bacon rashers
pinch allspice	1 bay leaf
pinch ground cloves	
½ teaspoon chopped fresh or pinch dried thyme	

1 Cut all the meat from the chicken; slice neatly.

Scrape the last pieces of chicken flesh from the bones (the bones can then be used for stock).
2 Mince the pork or veal and the meat from the giblets. Blend with the scraped chicken meat and add seasoning, spices and thyme.
3 Stir in the sherry or brandy and sufficient beaten egg to bind the forcemeat.
4 Line a large mould or terrine with bacon rashers and put in a layer of the forcemeat mixture. Place the bay leaf and slices of chicken on top, put on more forcemeat and finally top with the last rashers of bacon.
5 Press down well, cover with a lid or greased foil and stand in a baking tin in half its depth of water. Cook in a cool oven (150°C, 300°F, Gas Mark 2) for 3 hours, adding more water to the tin if necessary.
6 Remove the lid or foil from the mould or terrine, cover with a plate to fit and place a heavy weight on top. This will cause the fat to rise to the top. Leave overnight, then remove weight and plate and add more melted fat to seal.
7 The pâté may be left in the mould or terrine and cut as required, or turned out on to a dish with salad. It will serve a larger number of people as an hors d'oeuvre.

Stuffed avocados

you will need for 4 servings:

METRIC/IMPERIAL

175 g/6 oz cooked chicken	2 ripe avocados
50 g/2 oz Danish blue cheese	1–2 tablespoons lemon juice
4 tablespoons mayonnaise	salt and pepper
1 tablespoon chopped walnuts	

to garnish:
lettuce, lemon slices

1 Dice the chicken and cheese and blend with the mayonnaise and nuts.
2 Halve the avocados, sprinkle with the lemon juice and seasoning and fill with the chicken mixture.
3 Garnish with lettuce and lemon slices.

Tomato surprise

you will need for 4–8 servings:

METRIC/IMPERIAL

8 large tomatoes	salt and pepper
cooked giblets from 1 large chicken	4 tablespoons grated Cheddar
50 g/2 oz cooked ham	

to garnish:
parsley
½ cucumber, sliced
1 lettuce heart, shredded

1 Cut the tops from the tomatoes and set aside. Scoop out the pulp and chop this finely.
2 Chop the giblets and ham and mix with the tomato pulp; season well.
3 Fill the tomatoes with the mixture and top with a

layer of grated cheese, then place the 'lids' in position.

4 Garnish with parsley, sliced cucumber and shredded lettuce.

Soups

A chicken soup can be an interesting first course or even a light main meal. The basis for chicken soups, like so many others, is a good stock. Chicken or chicken bones produce an excellent stock, and there are various ways of making this.

After boiling chicken use the liquid in which the bird was cooked, which will provide an excellent flavoured stock. Another method is to make stock from the leftover chicken carcass. Where a really white stock is necessary, omit the dark intestines. If a slightly darker stock is required, brown the carcass in a little hot butter or chicken fat before adding the liquid.

To make the stock, cover the bones with water. Allow at least 1 hour simmering or a minimum of 20 minutes at High (15 lb) pressure if using a pressure cooker. A longer cooking period produces a better flavoured liquid.

A third method is to simmer the chicken giblets for 30–45 minutes or cook for 10 minutes at High (15 lb) pressure. Diced vegetables or mixed herbs (a bouquet garni) add interest to the stock. For a clear stock, strain before using.

Freezing soups

Soups freeze well on the whole, although if wine is added it will lose some flavour. Where cream is included in the ingredients, add this when reheating the soup if possible.

Thickened soups may become thinner as they thaw, so this stage may be better left until the soup is reheated, although it is comparatively simple to adjust the amount of flour or cornflour as you reheat the mixture. Most chicken soups have suggested freezer storage times of 6–8 weeks.

Chicken soup (1)

you will need for 4 servings:

METRIC/IMPERIAL

1 chicken carcass	salt and pepper
1 onion, sliced	water to cover
2 carrots, sliced	chopped parsley
2–3 peppercorns	25 g/1 oz long-grain rice
2 cloves	or alphabet noodles

1 Break up the chicken carcass and put it in a pan with the onion, carrots, peppercorns, cloves and seasoning.

2 Cover with water and simmer gently for 2 hours, or allow 30 minutes at High (15 lb) pressure.

3 Strain and add any leftover pieces of chicken meat, a little chopped parsley and the rice or noodles.

4 Simmer for 15 minutes more or 5 minutes at High (15 lb) pressure to cook the rice or noodles, then serve.

Chicken soup (2)

you will need for 4 servings:

METRIC/IMPERIAL

1 chicken carcass	300 ml/½ pint milk
1 litre 150 ml/2 pints chicken stock	1 tablespoon cornflour
	25 g/1 oz butter
100 g/4 oz cooked chicken meat	salt and pepper

1 Simmer the carcass in the stock for 1 hour or cook for 30 minutes at High (15 lb) pressure, then strain.

2 Add the cooked chicken meat and milk and cook for a further 15 minutes or 5 minutes at High (15 lb) pressure.

3 Rub through a sieve or liquidise and blend with the cornflour. Add butter and seasoning and reheat for 10 minutes, stirring well.

Variations:

Chicken and almond soup: Omit the cornflour at stage 3. Blend the chicken purée with 50 g/2 oz ground almonds. Return to pan, reheat and stir until thickened. Top with yogurt and blanched almonds.

Chicken and leek soup: After straining the stock at stage 1, add 4 large chopped leeks with the cooked chicken meat.

Chicken and vegetable soup: Add a mixture of vegetables to the chicken carcass at stage 1 halfway through the cooking.

Cream of chicken soup: Omit the cornflour at stage 3. Heat the butter in the pan, stir in 25 g/1 oz flour, then add the chicken purée. Bring to the boil, stirring until thickened, then blend in 150 ml/¼ pint single or double cream and heat through without boiling.

The following variations serve up to 6 people.

Cheddar chicken soup: Stir 75 g/3 oz grated Cheddar into the hot soup at stage 3 and heat gently but do not boil. To serve au gratin, spoon the soup into a flame-proof dish, top with rounds of toast and grated cheese and brown under the grill.

Hot chicken and avocado soup: Sieve or liquidise the pulp of 1 large avocado with the chicken at stage 3. Return to the pan with 2 teaspoons lemon juice. Reheat. Top with natural yogurt and chopped parsley before serving.

Cucumber and chicken soup: Sieve or liquidise a peeled chopped cucumber with the chicken at stage 3. To serve hot, reheat and top with yogurt and sliced cucumber. To serve cold add 150–300 ml/¼–½ pint yogurt to the cold cucumber and chicken purée and flavour with a little lemon juice.

Curried chicken soup: Slice 2 peeled onions and fry in 25 g/1 oz chicken fat or butter. Blend in 1 tablespoon curry powder and add to the purée at stage 3. Sprinkle the soup with a little grated fresh or desiccated coconut before serving.

Paprika soup: Blend 1 tablespoon paprika with the chicken purée at stage 3. Reheat and top the soup with hot tomato purée, natural yogurt and more paprika.

Chicken and potato soup

you will need for 4–6 servings:
METRIC/IMPERIAL

1 chicken carcass	salt and pepper
1 litre 150 ml/2 pints chicken stock	175 g/6 oz cooked chicken
225–350 g/8–12 oz potatoes, peeled and diced	300 ml/½ pint milk
	1 tablespoon cornflour
	25 g/1 oz butter

1 Simmer the carcass in the stock for 1 hour or cook for 20 minutes at High (15 lb) pressure.
2 Strain, then add the diced potatoes and seasoning and simmer for 15–20 minutes, or cook for 5 minutes at High (15 lb) pressure.
3 Add the cooked chicken meat and milk and cook for a further 15 minutes or 5 minutes at High (15 lb) pressure. Rub through a sieve or liquidise. Return to the pan.
4 Blend in the cornflour, add butter and seasoning to taste. Cook for 10 minutes, stirring.

Chicken tomato soup

you will need for 4 servings:
METRIC/IMPERIAL

350 g/12 oz tomatoes	1 tablespoon cornflour
1 chicken carcass	150 ml/¼ pint water
1 litre 150 ml/2 pints water or chicken stock	salt and pepper
175 g/6 oz cooked chicken, diced	4 tablespoons single cream

1 Skin and de-seed the tomatoes. Simmer with the chicken carcass in the water or stock for 1 hour or cook for 30 minutes at High (15 lb) pressure.
2 Sieve or liquidise then add chicken meat and the cornflour blended with the water. Bring to the boil and cook for 10 minutes.
3 Add seasoning and cream and serve; *do not reheat.*

Cock-a-Leekie

This is a good way to prepare two meals in one. Boil a whole fowl, use half the meat for this traditional soup and use the remainder in another dish. If preferred, make the soup using 2 chicken joints only and put all the meat in the soup.

serves 6–8

Simmer a boiling fowl plus the giblets in 2·25 litres/4 pints seasoned water until nearly tender. Add 450 g/1 lb sliced leeks and 50–75 g/2–3 oz long-grain rice and continue cooking until chicken is tender. Lift the bird out of the liquid and dice the required amount of meat from the fowl and giblets. Return the meat to the pan with a few diced cooked prunes if liked and reheat. Top with chopped parsley.

Chicken broth

you will need for 4–6 servings:
METRIC/IMPERIAL

25 g/1 oz pearl barley or long-grain rice	225 g/8 oz vegetables, finely diced
1 litre 150 ml/2 pints stock	little cooked chicken
	salt and pepper

to garnish:

chopped parsley	croûtons

1 If using barley, blanch first: put into cold water, bring water to the boil then strain. (Rice does not need blanching.)
2 Add blanched barley or rice to the stock with the vegetables and cook steadily for 15 minutes or 5 minutes at High (15 lb) pressure.
3 Add tiny pieces of cooked chicken and heat through for about 10 minutes or 1 minute at High (15 lb) pressure.
4 Add seasoning and garnish with parsley and croûtons.

Variations:

Chicken mushroom broth: Use only chopped onion and celery at stage 2. Add 50–100 g/2–4 oz thinly sliced mushrooms at stage 3.

Chicken noodle soup: Omit the barley or rice. Substitute 50 g/2 oz small noodles and cook for 10–12 minutes or under pressure as stage 2.

Portugaise soup: Use rice and add 4 medium skinned chopped tomatoes at stage 3.

Chicken and beef soup

you will need for 4–6 servings:
METRIC/IMPERIAL

1 boiling fowl	2 leeks
1 kg/2 lb shin beef	salt and pepper
2 onions	bouquet garni
2 turnips	water to cover

1 Put the cleaned fowl in a very large strong saucepan. Cut the meat into 3 or 4 large pieces, prepare and chop the vegetables and add to the pan.
2 Sprinkle with salt and pepper and put in the bouquet

garni. Cover the fowl completely with water and bring slowly to the boil.

3 Simmer very slowly for 2–3 hours or until the fowl is tender.

4 Remove fowl and pieces of meat from the pan and serve the soup; retain some of the soup to make a sauce for the boiled fowl (see page 17).

Note:
This recipe may sound extravagant, but it not only makes a wonderful soup but two delicious main dishes as well.

Chicken chowder

you will need for 4–6 servings:

METRIC/IMPERIAL	
450 g/1 lb uncooked chicken	1 onion, finely chopped
600 ml/1 pint water	3 potatoes, diced
2 rashers bacon	600 ml/1 pint milk
25 g/1 oz butter	salt and pepper

to garnish:
dried breadcrumbs

1 Cut the chicken into neat 1-cm/½-inch pieces and put into a saucepan with half the water; bring to the boil.

2 Lower the heat and simmer for 30 minutes or cook for 10 minutes at High (15 lb) pressure. Drain thoroughly, reserving the stock.

3 Cut the bacon into neat pieces, put into the saucepan and fry in its own fat until just pale brown.

4 Add the butter and when it is very hot put in the finely chopped onion and continue cooking until nearly soft.

5 Add the diced potatoes and the rest of the water and bring to the boil, cooking for 10 minutes.

6 Put in the reserved chicken stock, cooked chicken, milk and seasoning and simmer very gently for a further 20 minutes.

7 Top with breadcrumbs just before serving.

Note:
This chowder is a favourite American dish and is very appetising for a light supper meal.

Variations:
Chicken and corn chowder: Omit 1 potato and substitute 100 g/4 oz cooked or canned sweet corn at stage 6.

Chicken onion chowder: Use all the water at stage 1. Fry 3 finely chopped onions in 40 g/1½ oz butter with the bacon at stage 4. Omit the potatoes and stage 5 but continue as stages 6 and 7.

Chicken and prawn chowder: Use stock made by simmering the shells of prawns in place of water. Add 100 g/4 oz peeled prawns at stage 6.

Giblet soup

Giblets can be used in soup as well as providing a stock.

1 Wash the giblets and check that there are no green patches in the liver from the gall bladder.

2 Cover the giblets with 900 ml/1½ pints water, add seasoning, bouquet garni and any vegetables desired.

3 Simmer until tender; the time will vary with the age of the bird, but should take about 45 minutes to 1 hour or 20–30 minutes at High (15 lb) pressure.

4 Remove all the meat from the neck and dice this with the liver etc., or sieve or liquidise, and reheat in the stock.

5 Serve with croûtons of fried bread.

Variations:
Clear giblet soup: First brown the raw washed giblets in a baking tin in the oven or under the grill, then proceed to stage 4. Remove the giblets, vegetables and herbs from the stock. Add a little sherry to the strained stock and reheat. Garnish with the chopped liver and a chopped hard-boiled egg.

Chicken liver soup: Use chicken livers (sometimes obtainable frozen, as well as fresh) in place of giblets.

Cream of giblet soup: Add enough single or double cream at stage 4 to give a rich flavour (i.e. a minimum of 150 ml/¼ pint to each 600 ml/1 pint of purée).

Danish giblet soup: Strain the stock after stage 3 and return to the pan. Add 2 peeled diced apples and 50–75 g/2–3 oz cooked diced prunes to each 1 litre 150 ml/2 pints of stock. Simmer until the apples are tender, then add the diced giblet meat and reheat as stage 4. Flavour with 1 teaspoon vinegar or lemon juice and a little sugar to give a sour-sweet taste. If preferred, thicken the stock with a little flour or cornflour before returning the diced giblet meat to the pan.

Mulligatawny chicken soup: Use 1 litre 150 ml/2 pints water at stage 2. Peel and chop 2 medium onions. Heat 40 g/1½ oz chicken fat or butter in a pan. Fry the onions until golden, then blend in 1 tablespoon curry powder and 1 tablespoon flour. Add the meat from the giblets to the curry mixture at stage 4 with 1 tablespoon sultanas, a generous pinch sugar and 1 tablespoon desiccated or grated fresh coconut. Heat thoroughly. Add 25 g/1 oz rice 15 minutes before the end of the cooking time.

Winter soup

you will need for 4–6 servings:

METRIC/IMPERIAL	
1 litre 150 ml/2 pints chicken stock	2 medium potatoes
50 g/2 oz lentils	2 medium onions
50 g/2 oz oatmeal	150 ml/¼ pint milk
salt and pepper	100 g/4 oz cooked chicken, diced

1 Put the chicken stock into a pan with the lentils and oatmeal; season well. Leave to soak for 1 hour.

2 Simmer for 30 minutes or cook for 5 minutes at High

(15 lb) pressure and allow pressure to drop at room temperature.

3 Peel and dice the potatoes and onions, add to the soup and simmer for 25 minutes or cook for 5 minutes at High (15 lb) pressure.

4 Stir the milk and diced cooked chicken into the soup and heat through.

Party soups

The following soups make good special meals. One of the most delicious party soups is a clear consommé as it makes a light first course.

Consommé

serves 6

Use the chicken carcass plus giblets and add a portion of chicken to give a good flavour. Cover with water, add seasoning, vegetables and herbs if desired. Simmer for 1–2 hours to make the stock, strain carefully then boil rapidly in an open pan to reduce and produce a stronger taste. Flavour with a little sherry and serve hot, cold or jellied.

Variations:

Chicken tarragon soup: Prepare 1 litre 150 ml/2 pints consommé; add the chopped pulp of 3 skinned and de-seeded tomatoes and 1 tablespoon chopped tarragon. Heat for a few minutes.

Consommé jardinière: Prepare 1 litre 150 ml/2 pints consommé. Cut 175 g/6 oz mixed vegetables into small dice, add 50 g/2 oz peas then cook in the consommé for 12–15 minutes.

Consommé julienne: Prepare 1 litre 150 ml/2 pints consommé. Cut 175 g/6 oz carrots, onions, turnips or other vegetables into matchsticks and cook in the consommé for 10 minutes.

Danish chicken broth: Prepare 1·75 litres/3 pints consommé then prepare very tiny dumplings (see page 19). Dice a selection of vegetables weighing 225 g/8 oz. Cook the vegetables and dumplings in the boiling consommé for 15 minutes.

Meringue soup: Prepare 1 litre 150 ml/2 pints consommé and transfer to a large shallow pan. Whisk 2 egg whites until very stiff; season well. Drop spoonfuls of the meringue on to the boiling consommé. Poach for 1 minute then turn and poach on other side. Garnish with chopped parsley and chopped chives.

San Remo soup: Prepare 1 litre 150 ml/2 pints consommé. Add 3 medium raw grated carrots and 50 g/ 2 oz rice and cook for 15 minutes. Top with grated cheese.

Swedish queen soup: Prepare 900 ml/1½ pints consommé. Blend 2 egg yolks, 150 ml/¼ pint single or double cream and 2 tablespoons dry sherry; whisk into the hot, but not boiling, consommé. Add cooked chicken balls (see page 9) and heat gently for a few minutes.

Jellied consommé: Good strong chicken stock will form a jelly without using any gelatine, but if the weather is hot and the stock insufficiently strong then gelatine may be needed. Use 1 teaspoon to each 600 ml/1 pint stock.

The easiest method of dissolving gelatine is to soften it in 2–3 tablespoons cold liquid, e.g. stock, consommé, water etc. Then blend the gelatine with the hot liquid and stir over a gentle heat until dissolved. Allow to stiffen slightly. Pour into soup cups before set, or either whisk and spoon into soup cups or cut into small cubes. Garnish with yogurt and chopped parsley or chives and serve with wedges of lemon.

Note:

Add diced green pepper, cucumber or skinned tomatoes to vary.

Iced consommé: Add the gelatine to chicken stock if desired, cool then freeze lightly. If storing for some time in the freezer, remove and allow to soften slightly before serving. Serve when frosted lightly, topped with yogurt and rings of cucumber.

Buttermilk soup

you will need for 6–8 servings:

METRIC/IMPERIAL

½ large cucumber	salt and pepper
100 g/4 oz cooked chicken breast	1 teaspoon sugar
300 ml/½ pint chicken consommé	½–1 teaspoon made mustard
600 ml/1 pint buttermilk or yogurt	100 g/4 oz peeled prawns

to garnish:
chopped dill or parsley

1 Peel and dice the cucumber and cut the chicken into small pieces.

2 Blend with all the other ingredients, chill and serve garnished with the chopped dill or parsley.

Jellied Madrilène

you will need for 4–6 servings:

METRIC/IMPERIAL

900 ml/1½ pints chicken consommé	½ tablespoon tomato purée
2 teaspoons gelatine	2 tablespoons sherry
2 large tomatoes	salt and pepper
	150 ml/¼ pint yogurt

to garnish:
lemon slices

1 Heat the consommé and dissolve the gelatine in this. Skin and de-seed the tomatoes and add with the rest

of the ingredients except the yogurt to the consommé.

2 Heat for a few minutes, then sieve or liquidise, chill and blend in the yogurt.

3 Allow to set and spoon into soup cups; garnish with lemon slices.

Watercress bortsch

you will need for 4–6 servings:

METRIC/IMPERIAL
1 medium cooked beetroot	150 ml/¼ pint soured
1 bunch watercress	cream or single cream
900 ml/1½ pints chicken	plus 1 tablespoon extra
consommé	lemon juice
	1 tablespoon lemon juice
	salt and pepper

to garnish:
chopped chives

1 Peel and chop the beetroot and remove the leaves from the watercress. Discard the stems.

2 Liquidise all the ingredients together, chill and top with chopped chives.

Note:
If you have no blender then grate the beetroot and chop the watercress leaves. Mix all the ingredients together thoroughly.

Chasseur soup

you will need for 4–6 servings:

METRIC/IMPERIAL
3 medium tomatoes	salt and pepper
1 medium onion	100–175 g/4–6 oz cooked
50 g/2 oz mushrooms	chicken
25 g/1 oz chicken fat or	2 tablespoons sherry or
butter	white wine (optional)
1 litre 150 ml/2 pints	
chicken stock	

1 Skin the tomatoes, peel the onion, wash but do not peel the mushrooms; finely chop all the vegetables.

2 Heat the fat or butter in a pan and gently fry the vegetables for 5 minutes.

3 Add the stock and season well then simmer for 15 minutes.

4 Add the chicken meat and sherry or wine if desired and heat through.

Variation:
Soup Mexicano: Add a finely diced red pepper (discarding core and seeds) at stage 2 and flavour with a generous pinch of chilli powder.

Party chicken soup supreme

It is worthwhile making this soup, using a whole chicken or boiling fowl, if you are providing a dish for many people.

Put the whole or jointed chicken into a pan with water to cover, and a bouquet garni – the best herbs to choose when cooking chicken are lemon thyme, rosemary, parsley and a small sprig of marjoram. Add a few sliced vegetables if desired. Simmer gently until tender.

When cooked remove all the flesh from the bird. If you want a very white soup discard the skin. Strain the stock carefully. Rub the cooked chicken through a sieve or liquidise with some of the stock in a blender and mix with enough stock to give a coating consistency.

For each 1 litre 150 ml/2 pints purée allow 50 g/2 oz butter, margarine or chicken fat (if the stock has been allowed to cool), 50 g/2 oz flour and 600 ml/1 pint milk. Melt the fat, stir in the flour and gradually blend in the milk. Blend with the chicken purée and heat gently. Whisk 150 ml/¼ pint single or double cream with 2 egg yolks, add to the soup with a little sherry to flavour and reheat gently without boiling. Garnish with chopped parsley. This is a very sustaining soup, so a generous 150 ml/¼ pint would be sufficient for a small portion.

Queen soup

you will need for 4–6 servings:

METRIC/IMPERIAL
for chicken forcemeat balls:
100 g/4 oz cooked chicken	1 egg
breast	salt and pepper
25 g/1 oz butter	few drops cream

for soup:
900 ml/1½ pints chicken	150 ml/¼ pint double
stock	cream
2 egg yolks	2 tablespoons sherry
	salt and pepper

1 Mince the chicken or put into the blender to make a smooth purée then blend with the butter, egg, seasoning and just enough cream to bind.

2 Make into tiny balls and poach in boiling salted water for about 10 minutes.

3 Meanwhile heat the chicken stock, blend the egg yolks with the cream and whisk into the soup, and *simmer gently* for a few minutes.

4 Add the sherry and seasoning. Serve hot or cold topped with the chicken forcemeat balls.

Fried croûtons

Croûtons give a pleasant texture to both hot and cold soups. Cut bread into small dice and fry in hot butter or fat until crisp and golden. Drain on absorbent paper. Serve hot or cold. For garlic croûtons, toss in garlic salt.

Basic ways with chicken

Baked chicken

When you bake a chicken, as opposed to roasting one, you generally add ingredients other than fat. You do not, however, use much liquid, which is why the flavour is different from a casserole dish.

The dishes in this section can be prepared, cooked and then frozen, ready to reheat later. They should be used within 2–3 months. If pre-cooking the dishes take care *not* to over-cook the food, otherwise the chicken may become dry when reheated.

Note:
Garlic tends to lose flavour during freezing.

Baked chicken with bacon

you will need for 4 servings:

METRIC/IMPERIAL
4 joints frying chicken
salt and pepper

to garnish:
sprig of parsley

4 large or 8 small rashers bacon

1 Season the joints of chicken and wrap the rashers of bacon right round them so that the chicken is completely covered.
2 Bake for 40 minutes in the centre of a moderately hot oven (200°C, 400°F, Gas Mark 6). Garnish with parsley.

Variation:
Jamaican chicken: Press halved bananas against the chicken joints, wrap in bacon and bake as stage 2.

Savoury baked chicken

you will need for 4 servings:

METRIC/IMPERIAL
450 g/1 lb cooked chicken
2 eggs
150 ml/¼ pint chicken stock
150 ml/¼ pint milk

salt and pepper
½ teaspoon finely chopped parsley
generous pinch mixed herbs

1 Cut the chicken into neat fingers.
2 Beat the eggs and pour on the liquids. Add the seasoning, parsley and mixed herbs.
3 Put the chicken into a greased ovenproof dish and pour the egg mixture over; stand the dish in a baking tin of water.
4 Bake in the centre of a moderate oven (160°C, 325°F, Gas Mark 3) until the custard is set; serve hot.

Chicken Florentine

you will need for 4 servings:

METRIC/IMPERIAL
4 joints frying chicken
50 g/2 oz butter or oil
450 g/1 lb spinach
salt and pepper
4 tablespoons double cream

2 tablespoons soft breadcrumbs
2–4 tablespoons grated cheese

1 Fry the chicken in the hot butter or oil until just golden; do not overcook.
2 Meanwhile cook the spinach, strain and mix with the seasoning and cream.
3 Put in the base of an ovenproof dish and top with the partially cooked chicken, breadcrumbs and grated cheese.
4 Pour any butter or oil remaining in the pan over the top and bake for 30 minutes in the centre of a moderately hot oven (200°C, 400°F, Gas Mark 6).

Variation:
Chicken Egyptienne: Omit the spinach and put a layer of sliced fried aubergine under the chicken at stage 3.

Chicken en papillote

you will need for 4 servings:

METRIC/IMPERIAL
2 hard-boiled eggs
40 g/1½ oz butter
40 g/1½ oz soft breadcrumbs
1 small clove garlic, chopped

½ teaspoon salt
pinch pepper
1 tablespoon chopped parsley
4 joints frying chicken

1 Chop the eggs, melt the butter and mix with breadcrumbs, chopped garlic, seasoning and parsley.
2 Coat each chicken joint with this mixture, wrap in foil or place in a greaseproof paper bag and seal tightly. Bake in the centre of a hot oven (220°C, 425°F, Gas Mark 7) for 30 minutes.
3 Remove to the grill pan, open the foil or bag and grill steadily until golden brown.

Variation:
Chicken and pork: Substitute 225–350 g/8–12 oz pork sausagemeat for the egg mixture and coat the chicken with this at stage 2. Bake uncovered until cooked and golden brown.

Chicken pimiento

you will need for 4 servings:

METRIC/IMPERIAL
15 g/½ oz butter	salt and black pepper
2 onions	1 large sweet red pepper
4 joints young chicken	300 ml/½ pint yogurt

1 Grease an ovenproof dish with the butter.
2 Peel and boil the onions for 10 minutes then cut into rings and lay in the base of the dish. Place the chicken joints on top and season well.
3 Remove seeds and core from the pepper, cut into thin rings and lay on top of the chicken.
4 Pour yogurt over and bake for approximately 45 minutes, depending on size of joints, in the centre of a moderately hot oven (190°C, 375°F, Gas Mark 5).

Chicken Portugaise

you will need for 4 servings:

METRIC/IMPERIAL
4 joints frying chicken	salt and pepper
1 onion	25 g/1 oz grated cheese
2–3 tomatoes, sliced	50 g/2 oz butter

1 Put the joints of chicken into a buttered ovenproof dish.
2 Peel and slice the onion thinly, place on the top with slices of tomato, season and sprinkle over the grated cheese.
3 Put small pieces of the butter on top and bake for 45–50 minutes in the centre of a moderately hot oven (190°C, 375°F, Gas Mark 5).

Chicken in orange

serves 4

Brown 4 chicken joints in 50 g/2 oz butter, then transfer to a baking dish. Pour 300 ml/½ pint orange juice, blended with 1 grated onion and seasoning, over the chicken. Cover the dish and bake for 45 minutes in the centre of a moderate oven (180°C, 350°F, Gas Mark 4). Garnish with watercress and orange segments.

Herbed chicken

serves 4

Skin 4 joints frying chicken, brush with melted butter and sprinkle with chopped fresh herbs. Put into a buttered ovenproof dish and bake for 40 minutes in the centre of a moderately hot oven (200°C, 400°F, Gas Mark 6). Cover the dish with buttered foil for the first 25 minutes.

Maryland chicken

serves 4

Skin 4 joints frying chicken and coat first in seasoned flour, then in beaten egg and finally in dried crumbs. Put into a well buttered baking dish. Blend 50 g/2 oz butter, 2 tablespoons hot water and 1 tablespoon wine or lemon juice and season well. Bake the chicken for 40 minutes in the centre of a moderately hot oven (200°C, 400°F, Gas Mark 6). Baste with the butter mixture while cooking.

Garlic chicken

you will need for 4 servings:

METRIC/IMPERIAL
4 joints frying chicken	¼ teaspoon savory
75 g/3 oz butter or margarine	⅛ teaspoon black pepper
	50 g/2 oz potato crisps
1–2 cloves garlic, chopped	50 g/2 oz cornflakes
½ teaspoon salt	

1 Skin the chicken joints; combine the butter or margarine, finely chopped garlic, salt, savory and pepper in a shallow baking dish.
2 Place in a moderately hot oven (190°C, 375°F, Gas Mark 5) until the butter has melted.
3 Crush the crisps and cornflakes and mix together.
4 Dip the chicken pieces into the melted butter mixture then into the crumbs to coat thoroughly.
5 Arrange the chicken in a single layer in a large shallow ovenproof dish. Sprinkle the remaining potato crisps and cornflakes over the chicken and bake in the centre of a moderately hot oven (190°C, 375°F, Gas Mark 5) until the chicken is crisp and brown.

Boiled Chicken

All types of chicken can be boiled. The term 'boiling' is actually incorrect, for if the liquid boils rather than simmers the outside of the bird becomes overcooked before the inner flesh is tender.

Place the chicken in a large pan; if you want a lightly flavoured stock, cover with cold water or other liquid. If on the other hand you need a smaller amount of a more concentrated stronger flavoured stock, then use only enough water or other liquid to half cover the bird and smear the breast with butter to keep it moist.

Add seasoning to taste, dried or fresh herbs, plus onion and other vegetables to flavour the bird and stock. Be sparing with dried herbs as too large a quantity gives a slightly musty taste.

Instead of using water in which to cook the chicken, use half water and half dry cider; add a little red or white wine to the water; use the zest of lemon or add a little wine vinegar, lemon juice or ginger beer.

Boiling different types of chicken

If cooking a young frying or roasting chicken by this method, first bring the liquid to the boil and remove any grey bubbles that may form on the surface of the liquid. Check that the pan is tightly covered, lower the heat and simmer steadily (there should be gentle bubbling on the surface of the liquid) for 15 minutes per half kilo/per lb and allow 15 minutes over.

If cooking a young boiling fowl allow 30 minutes per half kilo/per lb and 30 minutes over.

If cooking a really old boiling fowl then use a very slow treatment. First put the bird into a large container. Then completely cover with water or other liquid and add seasoning to taste. Cover with a tightly fitting lid and simmer carefully *without boiling*, allowing 30 minutes per half kilo/per lb and 2 hours over. (Make sure the water has only an occasional bubble on the surface.)

Do not hurry the cooking of a boiling fowl, since this will make it tough. Slow cooking is the secret of success. It must be remembered that the age of the fowl will determine cooking time to some degree and it is therefore advisable to allow extra time, so that if by some unlucky chance you have a rather older bird, you can go on cooking longer than the recommended period.

Serving boiled chicken

If you intend to serve the boiled chicken cold, then allow it to cool in the liquid in the pan; since the bird will continue to soften a little as it cools, deduct 5–10 minutes from the total cooking time.

If you intend to serve the bird hot, lift it from the liquid. The easiest way to do this is to insert a long cooking fork or spoon inside the bird, lift it above the pan, tilt gently to let any liquid inside the body drain back into the pan, then put on to a warm serving dish.

In addition to serving boiled chicken as a dish, this method of cooking is ideal for making a salad or for use in dishes requiring cooked chicken.

Note:

The giblets of the chicken give a good flavour when cooked with the bird, but they do tend to darken the stock. In many recipes this does not matter. Use fat from the stock for cooking where recommended.

Using electric casseroles and pressure cookers

The modern electric casserole or slow cookers are good ways of 'boiling' chicken. It will need to be jointed in the case of most casseroles, which are too shallow for the whole bird. Follow the manufacturer's directions for cooking.

To boil a chicken in a pressure cooker put the bird into the cooker without the trivet. Spread butter over the breast of a young lean chicken. Add a minimum of 300 ml/½ pint water for a small young bird or 600 ml/1 pint for an older or larger bird. Never have the pan more than half filled with water. Add seasoning, herbs and vegetables to taste.

Bring up to High (15 lb) pressure and allow 5 minutes per half kilo/per lb for a young bird and up to 10 minutes per half kilo/per lb for an older boiling fowl. Reduce pressure under cold water.

Freezing boiled chicken

While you can boil a chicken, cool, then freeze it, there will be some loss of taste. It is better to freeze the raw chicken then *allow it to thaw out completely* and cook as above.

As boiling fowls often have a lot of yellow fat, it is better to remove this before wrapping the bird for freezing; excess fat reduces the storage time, as it becomes slightly rancid over a long period. Use the fowl within 12 months.

These simple dishes can be served with boiled or creamed potatoes, cooked rice or pasta.

Blanquette of chicken

Boil the chicken with the giblets, *except* the liver. Add several onions (each onion can be stuck with 2 cloves if desired), several carrots, seasoning and a bouquet garni. Cook until the bird is tender. Make a white sauce with 50 g/2 oz chicken fat, butter or margarine, 50 g/2 oz flour and 300 ml/½ pint milk. Gradually whisk in 300 ml/½ pint stock strained after cooking the chicken, season to taste and heat well; then add 2 egg yolks, blended with 4 tablespoons single or double cream, and heat without boiling. Joint or carve the chicken and coat with the sauce. Garnish with chopped parsley.

Boiled chicken suprême

Boil the chicken, adding vegetables only to flavour the stock (no additional vegetables are required for this dish). When cooked, slice or joint the chicken neatly and coat with Suprême sauce (see page 20).

Boiled chicken and vegetables

Boil the chicken. Add a few vegetables at the beginning of the cooking period to flavour the stock, but add the remainder later so they remain firm and a good colour. Arrange the cooked vegetables round the whole or carved bird, garnish with chopped parsley and either coat with a sauce or serve separately.

Dumplings

These are an excellent accompaniment to boiled chicken. Cook them in the pot with the chicken towards the end of the cooking time.

you will need for 4–6 servings:
METRIC/IMPERIAL
100 g/4 oz flour (with
  plain flour use 1
  teaspoon baking powder)
salt and pepper

50 g/2 oz shredded suet
2 teaspoons chopped
  parsley
water to mix

1 Sift dry ingredients. Add suet and parsley and mix to a fairly sticky dough with the water.
2 Bring the liquid in the pan to the boil. Check that there is enough liquid, as dumplings absorb an appreciable amount.
3 Roll the mixture into balls (remember they will swell upon going into the liquid) then drop into the liquid.
4 Cook steadily, uncovered, for 15–20 minutes until well risen (this period of steady boiling rather than simmering will not spoil the bird). The dumplings can be kept in the stock for a time before serving.

Variations:

Bacon: Fry or grill 2 rashers bacon, chop finely and add to the flour mixture before mixing with the water at stage 1.

Giblet: Add finely chopped liver and stomach meat from the bird before mixing with the water at stage 1.

Herb: Add 1–2 teaspoons mixed chopped fresh herbs or $\frac{1}{2}$–1 teaspoon mixed dried herbs with the parsley at stage 1.

Horseradish: Add up to 1 tablespoon finely grated fresh horseradish or 1–2 tablespoons horseradish cream before adding the water at stage 1.

Lemon: Add the grated rind of 1 lemon plus a little lemon juice before mixing with the water at stage 1.

Low-cholesterol: Use 1 tablespoon corn oil instead of the suet at stage 1.

Parsley: Use up to 1 tablespoon chopped parsley at stage 1.

Rich: Bind with an egg or 2 egg yolks plus a little water at stage 1.

Savoury: Use stock instead of water to bind at stage 1; the seasoning could include celery salt or garlic salt.

Tomato: Bind with tomato purée or tomato juice instead of water at stage 1.

Vegetarian: Use vegetable fat or margarine instead of suet at stage 1.

Dumplings for soup: Make the dumplings the size of a hazelnut at stage 3 and cook for about 10 minutes only.

Chicken in aspic

Use a good light chicken stock (made without the giblets).

to 600 ml/1 pint stock allow:
METRIC/IMPERIAL
1 small carrot
1 small onion
1 stick celery, diced
grated rind and juice of
  $\frac{1}{2}$ lemon
1 bay leaf
salt and pepper

$1\frac{1}{2}$ tablespoons white malt
  vinegar
$1\frac{1}{2}$ tablespoons white wine
  vinegar
3–4 tablespoons white
  wine or dry sherry
15 g/$\frac{1}{2}$ oz gelatine
1 boiling fowl

to garnish:
tomato

1 Put the stock into a pan, add the peeled carrot, peeled onion and diced celery then the rest of the ingredients except the gelatine and chicken and simmer for 10 minutes.
2 Strain through several thicknesses of fine muslin. To produce a perfectly clear liquid, add stiffly whisked white and shell of 1 large or 2 smaller eggs and simmer for another 10 minutes. (The egg whites and shells gather up any tiny particles of grease that might have come through the muslin.)
3 Strain then remove the egg whites and shells if used.
4 Measure the liquid and allow 15 g/$\frac{1}{2}$ oz gelatine to each 600 ml/1 pint, then dissolve the gelatine and blend to make the jelly. You will need about 900 ml/ $1\frac{1}{2}$ pints to give a good coating.
5 Boil, then skin the chicken and cool.
6 Allow the jelly to cool and become the consistency of a syrup. Brush one layer over the chicken, allow to set, then repeat with the remaining jelly.
7 Garnish with small pieces of tomato.

Chicken brawn

you will need for 8–10 servings:
METRIC/IMPERIAL
1 boiling fowl with
  giblets
2–4 pigs' trotters
$\frac{1}{2}$–1 lemon (optional)

bouquet garni
water to cover
salt and pepper

1 Put the fowl with the giblets, trotters and lemon rind, thinly pared, into a large pan and add the lemon juice, herbs, enough water to cover and seasoning.
2 Bring the water to the boil, skim and lower the heat; cover the pan and simmer gently for $2\frac{1}{4}$–$2\frac{3}{4}$ hours or until the chicken is very tender.
3 Lift the chicken, giblets and trotters out of the pan and dice the meat (discarding the stomach). Pack all the meat into a large basin or mould.
4 Boil the stock very fast in an open pan until only about 300 ml/$\frac{1}{2}$ pint remains; strain over the meat and leave to set.

Note:
Chopped celery, whole onions and carrots could be

added, but do not overcook, as they would spoil the clarity of the jelly.

Variations:

Poulet en gelée (1): If you like a soft jelly, omit the pigs' trotters. For a firmer jelly use 1–2 trotters. Use a roasting bird for this. Shorten cooking time at stage 2 to 1¼–1½ hours or until the bird is just tender. Lift the whole chicken out of the pan and place in a casserole (it should be a fairly good fit, leaving a small space all round). Boil the stock as stage 4 above, strain over the chicken and allow to set.

Poulet en gelée (2): Joint a roasting chicken and simmer as stage 2 until the chicken is just tender, about 35–45 minutes. Remove the chicken from the pan and pull away the bones. Pack the chicken meat into a dish. Boil the stock as stage 4, strain over the chicken and allow to set. This dish looks very attractive if diced carrots and peas are added to the pan towards the end of cooking then arranged with the chicken in the dish.

Chicken chaudfroid (1)

you will need for 4 servings:

METRIC/IMPERIAL
150 ml/¼ pint aspic jelly   4 joints cooked chicken
300 ml/½ pint mayonnaise

to garnish:
tomato

1 Make up the aspic jelly using instructions on the packet and when it is cool, but not set, add the mayonnaise (see page 80).
2 Coat the chicken joints with this sauce and when firm, garnish with small pieces of tomato.

Note:

If using chicken breast, remove skin. If using leg and thigh joints, take off skin and remove bones to give a neat shape.

Variation:

Chicken chaudfroid (2): Use half mayonnaise and half whipped cream at stage 1.

Chicken in horseradish cream sauce

you will need for 6–8 servings:

METRIC/IMPERIAL
1 boiling fowl
water to cover
salt and pepper
50 g/2 oz butter
50 g/2 oz flour
300 ml/½ pint milk

3 tablespoons freshly grated horseradish or 2 tablespoons horseradish cream
pinch sugar
2 teaspoons vinegar

1 Put the whole chicken into a large pan with water and seasoning to taste and cook for 15 minutes per half kilo/per lb, allowing 15 minutes over.
2 Lift the chicken out of the pan and let the liquid boil,

uncovered, until reduced, then strain off 300 ml/½ pint, return the chicken to the pan and keep hot in the remaining liquid.
3 Make a sauce with the butter, flour, the measured stock and the milk and cook until thickened and smooth. Add the horseradish, extra seasoning to taste, sugar and vinegar and keep hot, but do not boil.
4 Lift the chicken out of the liquid and serve warm with the sauce.

Lemon chicken

you will need for 6–8 servings:

METRIC/IMPERIAL
pared zest and juice of 1 lemon
1 large boiling fowl
225 g/8 oz small onions
225 g/8 oz small carrots
2–3 sticks celery
2–3 bay leaves
3 peppercorns
salt and pepper

50 g/2 oz mushrooms
50 g/2 oz butter
1 egg
4 tablespoons double cream
150 ml/¼ pint sherry
50–100 g/2–4 oz blanched almonds

1 Squeeze lemon juice over the outside of the fowl; put the pared lemon zest inside.
2 Peel the onions and carrots, chop the celery; place in a casserole with the chicken, bay leaves and peppercorns. Add water to within 2·5 cm/1 inch of the top, season and cover.
3 Cook until tender in the centre of a cool oven (140°C, 275°F, Gas Mark 1) (this gives the effect of boiling) then lift the chicken out on to a dish and keep hot.
4 Slice the mushrooms, melt the butter and fry until soft.
5 Beat the egg and cream together and gradually whisk in 300 ml/½ pint of the hot stock, pour into a pan and stir over a low heat until thickened.
6 Add the mushrooms, sherry and almonds and coat the chicken with the sauce. Serve with the cooked vegetables from the casserole.

Poulet suprême

you will need for 4 servings:

METRIC/IMPERIAL
2 large or 4 small cooked chicken breasts

for the suprême sauce:
25 g/1 oz butter
25 g/1 oz flour
300 ml/½ pint chicken stock
150 ml/¼ pint milk

to garnish:
1 hard-boiled egg
100–175 g/4–6 oz mushrooms

100–175 g/4–6 oz long-grain rice

2 egg yolks
2 tablespoons double cream
½ teaspoon lemon juice

25 g/1 oz butter
paprika
parsley

1 If using the breasts from a large chicken divide each one into 2 portions; cook the rice.
2 Meanwhile prepare the sauce: heat the butter in a pan, stir in the flour, then add the chicken stock and milk and bring to the boil; cook until it acquires a smooth slightly thickened consistency.
3 Whisk the egg yolks and cream and blend into the hot, but not boiling, sauce.
4 Add the chicken breasts and heat gently for 10 minutes; add the lemon juice.
5 Chop the egg; slice the mushrooms, melt the butter, fry until soft.
6 Put the rice on to a hot serving dish, top with the chicken and the sauce, then garnish with chopped egg, fried mushrooms, paprika and parsley.

Poulet en cocotte bonne femme

you will need for 6–8 servings:

METRIC/IMPERIAL
for the stuffing:

chicken liver	pinch mixed herbs
225 g/8 oz pork sausagemeat	

1 large roasting chicken or young boiling fowl	4–6 small potatoes
	600 ml/1 pint chicken stock
25 g/1 oz butter	1–2 bay leaves
1 tablespoon oil	bouquet garni
2–3 sticks celery	salt and pepper
few celery leaves	single or double cream (optional)
2 turnips	
6 carrots	

1 Chop the raw chicken liver and blend with the sausagemeat and herbs; put into the chicken.
2 Heat the butter and oil in a large saucepan and turn the chicken in this until golden brown.
3 Chop the celery and the leaves, peel and dice the rest of the vegetables and add to the chicken (reserving the potatoes) with the stock, herbs and seasoning.
4 Cover the pan, bring to the boil and simmer steadily for 1¼–1½ hours or until the chicken is nearly tender; add the potatoes and cook for a further 20–30 minutes.
5 Lift the vegetables (except the potatoes) on to a hot dish, carve the chicken and put it with the vegetables.
6 Mash the potatoes into the stock left in the pan or liquidise and return to the pan; stir in a little cream if liked and extra seasoning.
7 Coat the chicken with the sauce.

Braised Chicken

Braising is one of the most delicious ways to cook chicken, for it keeps the bird moist and tenderises older fowls. It is a connoisseur's method.

Often braising is confused with stewing. Braised foods are *not* cooked in a liquid, as with stewing, but first browned and then cooked above a selection of vegetables etc. known as a mirepoix. The classic definition of braise is to first brown the food in fat, then cook in moist heat (the moisture is provided by the vegetables and a tiny quantity of liquid). Once, when braising was done on top of the cooker, special braising pans made of heavy gauge metal were used, so there was little possibility of the foods burning. Today it is considered better to do most of the cooking in the oven, so the dish used must have a very well fitting lid or be covered with foil.

There is some similarity between braising and pot roasting, but generally small pieces of chicken are braised, whereas whole poultry is pot roasted. This method is ideal for turkey portions.

Making a mirepoix

For a mirepoix, choose a selection of diced root vegetables, plus chopped leek, chopped herbs and a little celery when in season. Bacon rinds or pieces of fat bacon are excellent for giving flavour to the mirepoix. While the mirepoix could be served round the cooked chicken, it is more usual to sieve or liquidise it and make it into a sauce to spoon over. No thickening would be necessary, for the root vegetables give the bulk desired. If you find the sieved or liquidised mixture a trifle thick, add a little stock or other liquid to reach the desired consistency. To prepare the chicken, first cut it into convenient portions. Then prepare the mirepoix. To braise chicken for 4 people, peel and dice 225–350 g/8–12 oz (prepared weight) root vegetables and add 1 sliced leek, 1–2 sticks diced celery and 1–2 tablespoons chopped parsley or other herbs (i.e. rosemary, tarragon or chervil) together with 1–2 rashers diced bacon (if liked). Naturally the flavour of the mirepoix can be varied according to the season.

Cooking braised chicken

Brown the chicken joints in a little fat. When golden remove them from the pan. Pour off any surplus fat (the mirepoix must not be put into a layer of fat in the pan).

Place the mirepoix into the cooking pan or an ovenproof casserole and season. Add about 5 tablespoons liquid to the mirepoix. This can be seasoned water, stock or red or white wine.

Lay the browned poultry on top of the mirepoix and season to taste. Cover the pan or ovenproof dish very tightly. It is essential to retain the moisture in the pan. If cooking on top of the cooker, lower the heat and cook gently until the chicken is tender. Naturally the time will vary with the age of the chicken.

Times and temperatures

Very tender young chicken joints should take from 35 minutes. Naturally this means the vegetables should be cut into sufficiently small pieces to cook in the same time.

Less tender poultry portions (i.e. old boiling fowl) should take about 2 hours. This may mean checking that the liquid does not completely evaporate during cooking.

If cooking in the oven, set the oven at moderate to moderately hot (180–190°C, 350–375°F, Gas Mark 4–5) for tender chicken or at cool (150°C, 300°F, Gas Mark 2) for less tender boiling fowl. Allow longer than for braising on top of the cooker (about one-third again extra cooking time). A whole younger chicken takes about 1½ hours, a whole boiling fowl about 3–3½ hours in a cool oven (140°C, 275°F, Gas Mark 1). Adjust the liquid as required.

Lift the cooked poultry on to a hot serving dish and sieve or liquidise the mirepoix (removing any bacon rinds if necessary). Add any extra stock, wine, water or even single cream to give the desired consistency. Heat again, spoon over the food and serve, garnished with toast or chopped herbs.

Braised chicken will lose flavour after freezing since it is not in liquid, as in a stew or casserole, but is above the mirepoix. Frozen chicken can be used for braising and there is then no need to defrost the jointed chicken before cooking.

The ingredients given in the recipes below take the place of the mirepoix previously described. Tender young chicken is used in all these dishes.

Chicken Bercy: Brown the chicken joints and brown about 450 g/1 lb sausages and 8 medium onions or shallots. Remove the chicken and add 100 g/4 oz large mushrooms. Pour in 5 tablespoons white wine or stock and replace the chicken.

Chicken with chestnuts and celery: Prepare and skin about 450 g/1 lb chestnuts (see page 44). Wash and chop a head of celery, together with a few of the celery leaves. Brown the chicken joints, remove from the pan and turn the chestnuts and chopped celery in any fat that remains. Add 5 tablespoons well seasoned chicken stock and the celery leaves. Replace the chicken joints and continue but do not sieve the mixture after cooking. Lift the chestnuts and celery from the pan with a slotted spoon, add a little more stock to the pan, heat and thicken. A few tablespoons double cream can be added to the thickened sauce if desired.

Chicken Lyonnaise

you will need for 4–6 servings:

METRIC/IMPERIAL

1 young boiling fowl	25 g/1 oz dripping or
salt and pepper	chicken fat
1 tablespoon oil	150 ml/¼ pint chicken
450 g/1 lb potatoes	stock
450 g/1 lb onions	2 tablespoons chopped
	parsley

1 Cut the chicken into neat pieces and season.

2 Heat the oil and fry the chicken pieces steadily until brown (there is generally enough natural fat on a boiling chicken for a small amount of oil to be enough).

3 Peel and slice the potatoes and onions thinly.

4 Spread the dripping or fat in the bottom of a casserole, add the potatoes and onions with the stock and parsley and season well.

5 Lift the chicken out of the pan and drain carefully so that no excess fat goes into the casserole.

6 Cover tightly and cook for nearly 2 hours in the centre of a cool oven (150°C, 300°F, Gas Mark 2).

7 Arrange the chicken joints on a dish with the vegetables round to serve.

Variations:

With herbs: Flavour the mixture of potatoes and onions with rosemary or tarragon at stage 4.

With courgettes: Substitute halved (but not peeled) courgettes, sliced tomatoes and onions for the potatoes at stage 4. Since courgettes soften quickly it is better to use a tender roasting chicken for the dish, not a boiling fowl, and to cook for only 1¼–1½ hours.

Chicken with sausages, beans and bacon: Use a young roasting chicken and cut into neat joints. Season and fry as stage 2, using the minimum of oil or fat; remove from the pan. Fry 4–8 sausages and 4 chopped bacon rashers for 4 minutes. Add a (447-g/15¾-oz) can baked beans and 150 ml/¼ pint beer or chicken stock. Replace chicken joints in the pan, cover and simmer on top of the cooker for 45 minutes.

Mexican chicken with brown sauce

you will need for 4–6 servings:

METRIC/IMPERIAL

1·75-kg/4-lb roasting	2 cloves garlic
chicken	1 tablespoon flour
salt and pepper	150 ml/¼ pint white wine
2 tablespoons oil	6 tablespoons chicken
12–18 shallots or small	stock
onions	25 g/1 oz plain chocolate

1 Cut the chicken into 4–6 neat joints and season well. Heat the oil, brown the chicken then lift it out of the pan.

2 Peel the shallots or onions and keep them whole; peel and chop the cloves of garlic.

3 Toss the shallots or onions with the garlic in any oil remaining in the pan, then stir in the flour; add the wine, chicken stock and the chocolate, broken into small pieces.

4 Replace the chicken joints on top of the onion mixture and cover the pan tightly.

5 Simmer gently for 45 minutes; check once or twice that there is sufficient liquid in the pan. Serve the dark brown sauce (which should not taste oversweet) over the chicken.

Variation:
Blend 1 tablespoon tomato purée into the wine and stock as well as the chocolate at stage 3.

Spiced chicken

you will need for 4 servings:
METRIC/IMPERIAL

4 joints frying chicken	salt and pepper
½ teaspoon ground cumin	50 g/2 oz butter
½ teaspoon ground coriander	450 g/1 lb young carrots
generous pinch ground cinnamon	1 large onion
	5 tablespoons chicken stock

to garnish:
lemon wedges	1 tablespoon chopped parsley

1 Skin the joints of chicken so they absorb the flavour of the spices and sprinkle with spices and seasoning.
2 Heat the butter in a pan and fry the chicken until golden brown; remove from the pan.
3 Peel and slice the carrots, peel and grate the onion and put into the pan with the stock and a little seasoning.
4 Place the chicken on top, cover the pan tightly and simmer for 30 minutes.
5 Garnish with lemon wedges and parsley.

Variations:

Chicken in tarragon: Sprinkle the chicken joints with freshly chopped tarragon and seasoning instead of the ground spices at stage 1.

Jugged chicken: Substitute port wine for stock at stage 3. Sieve or liquidise the vegetable mirepoix when cooked and reheat with a little stock plus 1–2 tablespoons redcurrant jelly. Serve with forcemeat balls (see page 37) and redcurrant jelly.

Fried Chicken

Fried chicken has become extremely popular in this country. It is essential to choose young chicken for this quick method of cooking. These are often sold as 'broiler' chickens. The birds have a delicate flavour so choose a sauce or accompaniments to complement them. Do not overcook fried chicken, or instead of being moist and delicious it will be dry and tasteless.

You can fry chicken from the frozen state unless you want to coat the portions; in this case it is better to defrost the chicken first. The joints of chicken should be well dried in absorbent paper or a clean cloth. Chicken can be fried without a coating or coated with seasoned flour for shallow frying; coated with a little seasoned flour then egg and crumbs for shallow or deep frying; coated with flour then batter for deep frying; or with flavoured coatings.

Freezing fried chicken
It is a pity to cook then freeze the chicken unless it is essential to do this. A better method is to coat the chicken, open freeze this and then pack. Fry from the frozen state if necessary, but thawing slowly does help to improve the flavour of the chicken. When the chicken is fried and then coated with sauce it freezes quite well.

Choosing fat for frying
The recommendation for the kind of fat to use for frying is not always the same. Sometimes butter is given, in other recipes a little oil is added to the butter. This is either because of the cooking time or ingredients used. Oil helps to prevent butter from burning.

In some recipes oil is the first ingredient listed for frying; in others fat is the first choice. The first-mentioned is the author's choice.

A number of interesting recipes for fried chicken with sauces are given on the following pages. But fried chicken may also be served with a salad, fried or grilled tomatoes and/or mushrooms and fried potatoes.

To coat with flour

you will need for 4 servings:
METRIC/IMPERIAL

25 g/1 oz flour	4 chicken joints
salt and pepper	

1 Put the flour and seasoning either into a paper bag or on a piece of greaseproof paper.
2 Drop the well dried pieces of chicken into the bag and shake well (this avoids any mess) or turn the joints round in the flour on the greaseproof paper.
3 Shake off any surplus flour before frying.

To coat with egg and crumbs

you will need for 4 servings:
METRIC/IMPERIAL

4 chicken joints	1 tablespoon water
salt and pepper	4 tablespoons fine soft or dried breadcrumbs
flour	
1 egg	

1 In order to give a good coating first dip the chicken joints in seasoned flour.
2 Blend the egg and water and brush over chicken.
3 Put the crumbs into a paper bag or on a piece of greaseproof paper.
4 Either shake the chicken joints in the bag until evenly coated or turn round in the crumbs on the paper, pressing these on to the chicken with a palette knife.
5 Shake off any surplus crumbs before frying.

To coat with batter

you will need for 4 servings:

METRIC/IMPERIAL
4 chicken joints   flour
salt and pepper

for the batter:
75 g/3 oz plain or   l egg
  self-raising flour   150 ml/¼ pint milk or
pinch salt   mixed milk and water

1 In order to help the batter stick, first coat the chicken with seasoned flour.
2 Sift the flour and salt together in a basin for the batter. Gradually add the egg and milk and beat until it becomes a smooth batter.
3 Lower the joints of chicken into the batter and turn until evenly coated.
4 Lift out and hold over the basin before frying so that any surplus batter drops back into the basin.

Flavoured Coatings for Chicken

The following flavourings can be added to the seasoned flour or breadcrumbs before coating the chicken for frying.

Lemon: Add the finely grated zest of 1–2 lemons; orange zest could be used instead.

Parsley: Add up to 1 tablespoon finely chopped parsley.

Parmesan: Add 25 g/1 oz grated Parmesan cheese.

Paprika: Add 1–2 teaspoons paprika.

Spice: Add up to 1 teaspoon mixed spice or grated nutmeg.

Curry: Add 1–2 teaspoons curry powder and a pinch sugar.

The following flavourings can be added to the beaten egg or batter coating.

Piquant: Add 1 teaspoon Worcestershire sauce and a few drops soy sauce.

Chilli: Add a few drops chilli or Tabasco sauce.

Lemon: Add 1 tablespoon lemon juice.

Tomato: Add 1 tablespoon tomato purée.

Mustard: Add 1–2 teaspoons made mustard.

To fry chicken in shallow fat

you will need for 4 servings:

METRIC/IMPERIAL
4 prepared chicken joints   75 g/3 oz butter, oil or
                        well-clarified dripping
                        or fat

1 Coat the joints of chicken as desired.
2 Heat the butter or other fat in a large open pan; you should have a depth of at least 1 cm/½ inch in the pan.
3 Put in the chicken and fry fairly quickly until brown on the underside then turn and brown on the second side; lower the heat and cook slowly to make sure the chicken is cooked through.
4 Drain on crumpled tissue or absorbent paper.

To fry chicken in deep fat

you will need for 4 servings:

METRIC/IMPERIAL
oil or fat   4 prepared chicken joints

1 Put only enough oil or fat into the pan to come halfway up the sides; if more is used it may overflow. Heat steadily. To test if the right heat has been reached lower a small cube of bread into the oil; it should turn golden brown in 1 minute. Do not allow the fat or oil to become any hotter, or the chicken will become too brown on the outside before being cooked through.
2 Coat the joints of chicken as desired.
3 Put the chicken joints into the oil or fat (they are easier to remove if a frying basket is used) and cook fairly quickly until golden brown.
4 Either lower the heat or remove the pan carefully from the heat and allow the chicken to continue cooking for a total of 12–15 minutes to make sure it is tender.
5 Drain on crumpled tissue or absorbent paper.

Chicken with walnuts

you will need for 4 servings:

METRIC/IMPERIAL
50 g/2 oz walnuts   300 ml/½ pint chicken
l small red pepper   stock
l small onion   15 g/½ oz cornflour
350 g/12 oz cooked   l teaspoon sugar
  chicken   l tablespoon soy sauce
4 tablespoons oil   2 tablespoons sherry

1 Break walnuts into large pieces; slice the red pepper, discarding core and seeds, and peel and slice the onion; cut the chicken into neat fingers.
2 Fry the walnuts, red pepper and onion in the oil until the vegetables are tender but not brown.
3 Stir in the chicken then add the stock.
4 Mix the cornflour and sugar with the soy sauce and

sherry. Add to the ingredients in the pan and simmer gently for 3 minutes, stirring constantly.
5 Serve hot with boiled rice.

Chicken Lychee

you will need for 4 servings:

METRIC/IMPERIAL

1 large onion	$\frac{1}{4}$ teaspoon ground cloves
2 tablespoons olive oil	10 black lychee seeds
25 g/1 oz butter	$\frac{1}{2}$ teaspoon chilli powder
4 joints chicken	$\frac{1}{4}$ teaspoon ground cumin
salt	$\frac{1}{4}$ teaspoon ground ginger
$\frac{1}{4}$ teaspoon ground	3–4 white lychees
coriander	300 ml/$\frac{1}{2}$ pint water or
$\frac{1}{4}$ teaspoon turmeric	chicken stock

1 Chop the onion and fry it in a mixture of oil and butter for 2–3 minutes.
2 Add the chicken with all the other ingredients except the water or stock.
3 Fry for 5–6 minutes until golden.
4 Add the water or stock; cook gently, uncovered, until the chicken is tender and some of the liquid has evaporated. Remove the lychee seeds (they look like stones). Serve with boiled rice.

Note:

Canned lychees may be substituted, in which case use some of the juice from the can instead of the lychee seeds.

Chicken meunière

you will need for 4 servings:

METRIC/IMPERIAL

4 joints frying chicken	$\frac{1}{2}$–1 tablespoon oil
salt and pepper	$\frac{1}{2}$ teaspoon lemon juice
75 g/3 oz butter	

1 Skin the chicken first if desired then sprinkle with seasoning. Fry steadily in hot butter and oil until the chicken is tender, about 20 minutes.
2 Lift out of the pan; allow the butter to brown, then add the lemon juice. Pour over the chicken. Serve with salad.

Fried chicken in white wine

you will need for 4 servings:

METRIC/IMPERIAL

4 joints frying chicken	75 g/3 oz butter and oil
salt and pepper	150 ml/$\frac{1}{4}$ pint white wine
15 g/$\frac{1}{2}$ oz flour	150 ml/$\frac{1}{4}$ pint chicken
1 small onion or 2 shallots	stock

1 Coat chicken with seasoned flour; peel and chop onion or shallots.
2 Heat butter and oil and fry chopped onion or shallots for 1–2 minutes.

3 Put in the chicken and fry until golden brown on both sides. Add wine and stock and continue cooking for approximately 15 minutes.
4 Serve with boiled rice or ribbon noodles.

Variations:
Normandy fried chicken: Peel and slice 2 dessert apples and fry with the onion or shallots at stage 2. Substitute cider for white wine at stage 3.

Provençal fried chicken: Add 1–2 crushed cloves of garlic and 2 large skinned sliced tomatoes at stage 2.

Fried chicken tartare

you will need for 4 servings:

METRIC/IMPERIAL

25 g/1 oz flour	50 g/2 oz oil or butter
salt and pepper	and oil
4 joints frying chicken	

for hot sauce:

300 ml/$\frac{1}{2}$ pint white	1 teaspoon chopped
sauce (see page 41)	gherkin
2 egg yolks	1 teaspoon chopped
1 tablespoon cream	parsley
1 tablespoon capers	$\frac{1}{2}$ teaspoon lemon juice

for cold sauce:

1 teaspoon chopped	150 ml/$\frac{1}{4}$ pint mayonnaise
gherkin	(see page 80)
1 teaspoon chopped	chopped fresh tarragon
capers	or few drops tarragon
1 teaspoon chopped	vinegar
parsley	

to garnish:

lettuce or watercress	lemon slices

1 Flour and season the chicken joints.
2 Fry in hot oil or butter and oil until tender.
3 For the hot sauce, whisk the white sauce with the egg yolks, cream, capers, gherkin and parsley. Cook gently for a few minutes without boiling. Add the lemon juice.
4 For the cold sauce, add the chopped gherkin, capers and parsley to the mayonnaise with the tarragon if available or tarragon vinegar.
5 Arrange the chicken on a bed of crisp lettuce or watercress. Garnish with slices of lemon.
6 Serve hot or cold with the appropriate sauce.

Madeira chicken

you will need for 4 servings:

METRIC/IMPERIAL

4 joints chicken	300 ml/$\frac{1}{2}$ pint Madeira
salt and pepper	wine or 150 ml/$\frac{1}{4}$ pint
15–25 g/$\frac{1}{2}$–1 oz flour	Madeira and 150 ml/
50–75 g/2–3 oz oil or	$\frac{1}{4}$ pint chicken stock
butter and oil	

1 Coat joints of chicken with seasoned flour.

2 Fry steadily in hot oil or butter and oil until crisp and brown. Lift on to a hot dish and keep hot.

3 Add the Madeira to the pan and stir until well blended with the fat remaining in the pan. Simmer for 8–10 minutes, strain and serve over the chicken.

Mushroom-stuffed chicken

you will need for 4 servings:
METRIC/IMPERIAL
for the stuffing:

100 g/4 oz mushrooms or mushroom stalks	l tablespoon soft breadcrumbs
2 teaspoons chopped parsley	l egg
25 g/l oz butter or margarine	salt and pepper
	4 legs frying chicken

to coat:

salt and pepper	l egg
flour	dried breadcrumbs

to fry:
fat or oil

1 Chop the mushrooms or mushroom stalks very finely. Blend with the parsley and the melted butter or margarine, crumbs and egg. Season well.

2 Split the flesh of the chicken and remove the bones: insert the tip of a really sharp knife into the flesh, cut down firmly, then work the knife round the bones and you will find they come out without any difficulty.

3 Press the stuffing in place of the bones, then roll the stuffed legs in seasoned flour, egg and crumbs. Fry in fat or oil for approximately 20–25 minutes. It is easier if you can use deep fat, but if you have 1 cm/½ inch fat, turn the joints from time to time. Do not fry too quickly, as the heat has to penetrate and cook the mushroom stuffing and the flavour is better if this mushroom mixture is not pre-cooked.

4 Serve hot with brown or mushroom sauce (see pages 42 and 41) and mixed vegetables, or cold with crisp lettuce.

Variation:
Savoury stuffed chicken: Peel or skin and chop medium onions and 2 medium tomatoes. Fry until soft in 50 g/2 oz butter, then add 50 g/2 oz chopped raw mushrooms and the rest of the stuffing ingredients at stage 1.

Note:
You could fry the stuffed chicken until just crisp on the outside, then transfer to a moderate oven (160°C, 325°F, Gas Mark 3) for about 25 minutes to complete the cooking.

Fried chicken breasts Alexandra

you will need for 4 servings:
METRIC/IMPERIAL

300 ml/½ pint white sauce (see page 41)	salt and pepper
75 g/3 oz cheese	75 g/3 oz butter
4 small chicken breasts or 2 breasts from a large young bird	4 slices bread
	150 ml/¼ pint cream

1 First prepare the white sauce; grate cheese and put to one side.

2 If using large breasts, divide each into 2 joints; season well.

3 Heat 25 g/1 oz butter in a frying pan and fry the bread until crisp and golden on both sides; put on a hot flameproof dish.

4 Add the rest of the butter to the pan, heat and fry the chicken breasts until pale golden on both sides. Add the cream and continue cooking gently for 10–15 minutes until tender.

5 Lift the chicken on to the fried bread.

6 Blend the cream from the frying pan and the grated cheese with the sauce.

7 Coat each breast with a little sauce and brown under a hot grill. Serve the rest of the sauce separately.

Variation:
Chicken à la York: Split the breasts (see page 28) and insert thin slices of ham spread with mustard.

Fried chicken Espagnole

you will need for 4 servings:
METRIC/IMPERIAL

economical or rich Espagnole sauce (see page 42)	4 joints chicken
	flour
	salt and pepper

to fry:
oil or fat

1 Make the sauce first as it takes longer to cook than the chicken. Prepare and fry the chicken joints; when cooked serve with the Espagnole sauce.

Variations:
Ham sauce: Add 2 chopped gherkins and 50–75 g/2–3 oz cooked diced ham to the Espagnole sauce just before serving. Pour the sauce round the chicken and serve.

Mushroom cream sauce: Fry the chicken using a rather generous 75 g/3 oz butter or butter with a little oil; when nearly tender add 100 g/4 oz thinly sliced mushrooms, 150 ml/¼ pint double cream and 4 tablespoons chicken stock. Simmer until the chicken and mushrooms are tender.

Fried chicken Americano

you will need for 4 servings:

METRIC/IMPERIAL

salt and pepper
4 joints chicken
4 small onions
50 g/2 oz oil or butter
  and oil

4 large tomatoes
150 ml/¼ pint white wine
  or chicken stock

to garnish:
chopped parsley

1 Season the chicken joints; peel and slice the onions thinly.
2 Heat the oil or butter and oil and fry the chicken and onions together for nearly 10 minutes until both are golden brown.
3 Skin and slice the tomatoes, add them to the pan with the wine or stock and simmer gently for a further 10–15 minutes until the chicken is tender.
4 Garnish with chopped parsley and serve with vegetables, boiled rice or pasta.

Variation:
Fried chicken chasseur: Add 50 g/2 oz thinly sliced mushrooms at stage 3.

Fried chicken with orange sauce

you will need for 4 servings:

METRIC/IMPERIAL

50 g/2 oz crushed
  cornflakes
½ teaspoon ground ginger
½ teaspoon salt

¼ teaspoon pepper
4 joints chicken
flour
1 egg

to fry:
oil

for the sauce:
grated rind of 1 orange
2 tablespoons orange juice
1½ tablespoons sugar

3 tablespoons redcurrant
  jelly

to garnish:
1 orange

1 Mix the crushed cornflakes, ginger, salt and pepper together.
2 Dry the chicken joints, dip in flour then into beaten egg and coat with the cornflake mixture.
3 Heat 2·5 cm/1 inch oil in a frying pan.
4 Place the chicken joints in the hot oil and fry until tender.
5 Beat the orange rind, juice, sugar and redcurrant jelly together but do not heat.
6 Cut the unpeeled orange into segments. Top the fried chicken with the orange segments and the sauce.
The following recipes all give a piquant taste to fried chicken. Naturally the amount of pepper or mustard must be varied according to personal taste. Remember that cayenne pepper is very hot, so use sparingly for the first time.

Chicken livers and kidneys in sherry

you will need for 4 servings:

METRIC/IMPERIAL

4 lambs' kidneys
12 chicken livers
75 g/3 oz butter
1 tablespoon flour
salt

¼ teaspoon pepper to taste
⅛ teaspoon grated nutmeg
pinch cayenne pepper
¼ teaspoon thyme
4 tablespoons sherry

1 Skin kidneys, remove cores and any white membrane, and wash, dry and cut into thin slices. Wash and dry chicken livers and cut in halves.
2 Melt the butter in a heavy pan and fry the kidneys and livers over high heat for 4–5 minutes; shake the pan frequently and turn the pieces to cook on each side.
3 Sprinkle in the flour, seasoning, spices and thyme and stir until the flour browns. Add the sherry and continue cooking until the gravy is smooth.
4 Serve on boiled rice or toast.

Devilled fried chicken

you will need for 4 servings:

METRIC/IMPERIAL

4 tablespoons flour
salt to taste
2 teaspoons dry mustard
pinch cayenne pepper
4 joints chicken

1 egg
1 tablespoon water
8 tablespoons fine
  semolina

to fry:
oil, vegetable fat or lard

1 Mix flour, salt, mustard and cayenne in a paper bag, drop each chicken joint into the bag and shake until well coated.
2 Dip pieces in egg beaten with the water and drain well in a sieve or colander. Allow to stand for 15–20 minutes until the egg mixture gets tacky.
3 Coat with the semolina, let stand again for a few minutes and shake off surplus semolina.
4 Heat 5 cm/2 inches fat until hot. Brown chicken pieces quickly on each side, then lower the heat and continue cooking until tender.
5 Serve hot or cold with vegetables or boiled rice, or cold with salad.

Variations:
Use dried breadcrumbs instead of semolina at stage 3. There is no need when using breadcrumbs for the chicken to stand at stages 2 and 3.

Curried fried chicken: Use only ½ teaspoon dry mustard and 1–2 teaspoons curry powder at stage 1. Coat in egg and water then with crisp breadcrumbs blended with a small amount of curry powder at stage 3.

Fried chicken diable

you will need for 4 servings:

METRIC/IMPERIAL
for sauce diable:

I onion	I tablespoon tomato
I carrot	ketchup
50 g/I2 oz mushrooms	I–3 teaspoons made
25 g/I oz fat or dripping	mustard
25 g/I oz flour	3 teaspoons
600 ml/I pint chicken	Worcestershire sauce
stock or water	generous pinch cayenne
pinch ground mace	pepper
celery salt and pepper	
flour	4 joints chicken
salt and pepper	
to fry:	*to garnish:*
50 g/2 oz oil or butter	watercress
and oil	

1 Peel and slice the onion and carrot and slice but do not peel the mushrooms.
2 Melt the fat or dripping and fry the onion slowly until golden brown. Add the flour and cook until lightly browned, stirring occasionally.
3 Pour in the stock or water and bring to the boil, stirring all the time, then add the rest of the sauce ingredients. Cover the pan and simmer for 30–40 minutes, stirring occasionally.
4 Sieve or liquidise the mixture for a thick sauce or strain if a thinner sauce is desired.
5 Flour and season the chicken joints lightly and fry in the hot oil or butter and oil, turning frequently to brown, for 10 minutes.
6 Lower the heat and cook the chicken gently for a further 10–15 minutes until cooked through and tender. Garnish with watercress and serve with the sauce.

Peppered fried chicken (1)

you will need for 4 servings:

METRIC/IMPERIAL

4 joints chicken	15–25 g/½–I oz flour
salt and pepper	12 peppercorns
to fry:	*to garnish:*
oil or fat	watercress

1 Skin the joints of chicken, coat in seasoned flour, then crush the peppercorns and press into the flour coating.
2 Heat the oil or fat and fry the chicken until crisp and golden brown.
3 Garnish with watercress and serve hot.

Variations:
Peppered fried chicken (2): Lift the chicken out of the pan and keep hot. Stir 150 ml/¼ pint single or double cream into the frying pan with 2–3 tablespoons brandy. Heat gently then spoon over the chicken before serving.

Fried chicken poivrade: Coat the chicken using only 4–5 crushed peppercorns. Fry and serve with poivrade sauce (see page 42).

Chicken Cordon Bleu

you will need for 4 servings:

METRIC/IMPERIAL

2 large or 4 small very	4 slices ham
tender chicken breasts	4 slices Gruyère cheese
to coat:	
salt and pepper	50 g/2 oz dried
15–25 g/½–I oz flour	breadcrumbs
I egg	
to fry:	
50–75 g/2–3 oz butter	I tablespoon oil
to garnish:	
lemon wedges	parsley

1 Cut the 2 large breasts in half down the middle but do not slice them too thinly at this stage.
2 Make a slit in each breast to form a large pocket or halve across the breast to give thinner slices.
3 Either insert a slice of ham and cheese into each pocket or make sandwiches of the chicken, then ham, then cheese and the last slices of chicken; be sure the ham and cheese are completely inside the chicken.
4 Coat the portions with seasoned flour, then beaten egg and breadcrumbs.
5 Heat the butter and oil and fry the chicken quickly to brown on either side, then lower the heat and continue cooking until the chicken is tender; do not overcook or the cheese will become tough. Drain on absorbent paper if a dry coating is preferred.
6 Serve garnished with wedges of lemon and parsley. This is very good served with a spiced tomato sauce (see page 43).

Variations:
Chicken with cream cheese and peppers: Blend 75–100 g/3–4 oz cream cheese with 2 tablespoons chopped red pepper and the same amount of chopped green pepper. Substitute this filling for the ham and cheese at stage 3.

Fried chicken with pâté: Fill the chicken with a home-made pâté (see page 9) or commercially prepared liver pâté at stage 3.

Stuffed chicken in cream sauce: Omit the egg and crumbs at stage 4. Lift chicken from the pan when cooked, then add 300 ml/½ pint single cream to the pan and stir well to absorb the juices. Add 1 tablespoon chopped parsley and a little seasoning. Pour over the chicken and serve.

Note:

This recipe is ideal for special occasions. To prevent the need for last-minute frying, brown the chicken earlier, then put in a baking tin and allow about 20 minutes above the centre of a moderately hot oven (200°C, 400°F, Gas Mark 6).

Norwegian parsley chicken

serves 4

Season 4 joints frying chicken and fry in 100 g/4 oz butter until nearly tender; add 4–6 tablespoons chopped parsley and continue cooking. Heat a small amount of cream in the pan just before serving if liked and pour over the chicken.

German fried chicken

serves 4

Coat 4 joints frying chicken with seasoned flour, beaten egg and equal quantities of soft breadcrumbs and grated Parmesan cheese. Fry in 100 g/4 oz butter until tender. Remove from the pan and fry 100 g/4 oz sliced mushrooms in the butter remaining in the pan. Add 150 ml/¼ pint double cream or béchamel sauce (see page 41), 4 tablespoons white wine, 1 tablespoon white wine vinegar and a beaten egg or egg yolk. Heat gently and serve with the chicken.

Cheddar fried chicken

you will need for 4 servings:

METRIC/IMPERIAL

flour	3 tablespoons dried
4 joints chicken	breadcrumbs
salt and pepper	3 tablespoons grated stale
½ teaspoon made mustard	Cheddar cheese
1 egg	

to fry:
oil or butter and oil

1 Flour chicken joints lightly. Blend the seasoning and mustard with the egg and use to brush chicken joints.
2 Mix the crumbs with the cheese and roll the chicken in this until completely covered.
3 Fry in either shallow or deep oil or butter and oil until tender.
4 Serve with a crisp green salad.

Garlic balls

These balls make an interesting accompaniment to fried or roasted chicken. They can be added to the pan in which the chicken is fried or to the grill pan during the process of cooking chicken or put round the chicken in the roasting tin. Turn once during cooking to crisp evenly.

you will need for 4 servings:

METRIC/IMPERIAL

1–2 cloves garlic	paprika
225 g/8 oz breadcrumbs	50 g/2 oz butter
1 teaspoon chopped	2 teaspoons chopped
parsley	onion
salt and pepper	milk or egg yolk
1 teaspoon chopped	dried breadcrumbs
mixed herbs	

1 Peel and crush the garlic and mix with the breadcrumbs, parsley, seasoning, herbs, paprika, softened butter and onion. Bind together with a little milk or egg yolk.
2 Form into acorn size balls and roll in dried breadcrumbs.

Grilled Chicken

Chickens for grilling, like frying, must be young as the object is to cook the chicken quickly.

It is advisable in view of the thickness of the flesh to put the chicken into the grill pan rather than on the grid unless you are able to place the pan well below the heat.

Pre-heat the grill; this will help the outside of the chicken to start cooking immediately.

Cook quickly on either side to brown, then lower the heat to make sure the chicken is cooked through to the middle. As you turn the chicken it should be well basted with plenty of melted butter, oil or a marinade or basting sauce. Use at least 50 g/2 oz butter to 4 portions of chicken. The average cooking time for grilling chicken is 15–20 minutes.

Using frozen chicken

Grilled foods should be served as soon as possible after cooking, so do not grill then freeze chicken unless you want to serve it cold later. Frozen chicken can be grilled without defrosting. However, if you require flavours to penetrate the flesh it is better to allow the joints to thaw out, then drain and dry well; then add the flavouring or put into a marinade.

The most usual accompaniments to grilled chicken are grilled or fried tomatoes and a green salad, but cold Tartare sauce (see page 80) or Maître d'hotel butter (see page 31) could also be served.

Spatchcock of chicken

To cook spatchcock of chicken, split a young bird down the underside and spread out flat, then grill. Allow a small poussin for 1 or 2 portions; a larger bird can be divided into 4 portions after cooking.

Spatchcock of chicken jardinière: Make 300 ml/½ pint brown sauce (see page 42). Cook a mixture of diced spring vegetables (carrots, turnips etc.), arrange the cooked chicken on a dish and garnish with the vegetables; coat with brown sauce.

Orange spatchcock: Blend the finely grated zest from 2 oranges with 50 g/2 oz well seasoned melted butter. Brush the chicken with this and grill. Squeeze 2–3 tablespoons orange juice over the chicken just before the end of cooking time. To give an attractive glaze to the chicken, sprinkle 1–2 teaspoons sugar over the skin before adding add the orange juice.

Spatchcock with sour cream sauce: Gently heat 300 ml/½ pint dairy soured cream blended with 2 egg yolks and season well. Pour over the chicken before serving.

Marinade for chicken (1)

you will need for 4 servings:

METRIC/IMPERIAL
for marinade:

2 teaspoons dry mustard	4 tablespoons wine
4 tablespoons cider	vinegar
pinch pepper	2 tablespoons olive oil
½ teaspoon salt	

4 chicken joints

1 Blend the mustard with a spoonful of the cider. Add pepper, salt, remaining cider and wine vinegar and gradually whisk into the oil.
2 Spoon over the chicken joints and leave to stand for at least 15 minutes, preferably 1 hour or longer.
3 Lift the chicken out of the marinade and grill, spooning the marinade over the chicken as it cooks.

Variations:

Marinade (2): Mix together 2 tablespoons white wine or cider vinegar, 2 tablespoons olive oil, a pinch garlic salt, pinch curry powder or cayenne and seasoning and soak the chicken joints in this as stage 2.

Marinade (3): Mix together 2 tablespoons olive oil, 2 tablespoons melted redcurrant jelly and 2 tablespoons vinegar. Soak the chicken joints in this as stage 2.

Marinade (4): Blend 2 tablespoons red wine and 2 tablespoons olive oil with seasoning and chopped garlic and soak the chicken joints in this as stage 2.

Flavouring grilled chicken

The following are suggestions for simple ways to flavour and serve grilled chicken. Barbecue recipes (see pages 34 and 35) can also be adapted for grilling.

Anchovy chicken: After grilling the chicken cover with a lattice of well drained anchovy fillets; heat under the grill for 1 minute.

Grilled chicken au gratin: Grill the chicken until just cooked. Blend 25 g/1 oz butter or margarine with 50 g/2 oz soft breadcrumbs and 50 g/2 oz grated cheese. Spread over one side of the chicken and grill for 2–3 minutes until brown.

Lemon chicken: Sprinkle the raw chicken with lemon juice and seasoning before grilling. Blend the finely grated zest of 1 lemon with 50–75 g/2–3 oz butter and use to baste the chicken during cooking.

Smothered chicken: Baste the chicken with plenty of seasoned butter while grilling. When the chicken is cooked (but not overcooked) spread with well seasoned whipped double cream and grill for a further 2–3 minutes. Soured cream (or double cream flavoured with lemon juice) could be used instead for a more piquant taste.

Swiss chicken: Spread the chicken with soft Swiss cheese after cooking and grill for a further 2–3 minutes.

Chicken Hollandaise

serves 4

Melt 50 g/2 oz butter, add seasoning and grill 4 joints chicken (preferably all breasts), keeping it well basted with the butter during cooking. Serve the chicken topped with Hollandaise sauce (see below).

Hollandaise sauce

you will need for 4 servings:

METRIC/IMPERIAL

2 egg yolks	50–100 g/2–4 oz butter
pinch cayenne pepper	
salt and pepper	
1–2 tablespoons white wine vinegar or lemon juice	

1 Put the egg yolks, cayenne and other seasoning into a heatproof basin and stand it over a pan of hot but not boiling water.
2 Whisk until thick and creamy, then gradually whisk in the vinegar or lemon juice.
3 Add the butter in small pieces, according to the richness desired. Do not add the butter too quickly or the sauce will become greasy.
4 Serve hot or cold; if serving cold, whisk as the mixture cools.

Variation:

Mousseline sauce: Use only 25 g/1 oz butter at stage 3 and flavour with a little grated nutmeg. Cool, then fold in 2–3 tablespoons whipped cream.

Chicken Béarnaise

serves 4

Melt 50 g/2 oz butter, add seasoning and grill 4 joints chicken, keeping it well basted with the butter while cooking. Serve with Béarnaise sauce (see below).

Béarnaise sauce

you will need for 4 servings:
METRIC/IMPERIAL

2 tablespoons white wine vinegar	1 bay leaf
1 shallot	2 egg yolks
1 teaspoon chopped tarragon	pinch cayenne
1 sprig thyme	salt and pepper
	50–100 g/2–4 oz butter

1 Before making the sauce put the wine vinegar into a pan; peel and chop the shallot and put it into the vinegar with the herbs.
2 Heat the vinegar for 2 minutes then leave it to stand in a warm place for about 5 minutes. Strain the vinegar.
3 Mix the egg yolks with the cayenne and other seasoning into a heatproof basin. Stand it over a pan of hot but not boiling water.
4 Whisk until thick and creamy, then gradually whisk in the strained vinegar.
5 Add the butter in small pieces, according to the richness desired. (Do not add the butter too quickly.)

Variation:
Choron sauce: Add 1 tablespoon tomato purée to the thickened Béarnaise sauce.

Soufflé chicken Mousseline

serves 4

First prepare Mousseline sauce (see Hollandaise sauce, page 30). Grill 4 joints chicken, basting with 50 g/2 oz seasoned butter. When the chicken is nearly cooked, whisk 2 egg whites, season and blend in 50 g/2 oz finely grated Gruyère or Parmesan cheese (the latter gives a stronger flavour). Put the cooked chicken portions into a flameproof dish and top with the meringue mixture. Brown under a very low grill or heat for 10 minutes in a cool oven (140°C, 275°F, Gas Mark 1). Serve the chicken piping hot with the cold Mousseline sauce.

Maître d'hôtel (parsley) butter

Flavoured butters should be put on the chicken just before serving. The butter should be very hard so it retains its shape as the dish is served. The butter gives an attractive appearance and moist flavour to either grilled or boiled chicken.

you will need for 4 servings:
METRIC/IMPERIAL

50 g/2 oz butter	lemon juice
2 tablespoons chopped parsley	salt and pepper

1 Cream the butter with the other ingredients.
2 Form into small balls, pats or squares and chill.

Variations:
Lemon butter: Omit the parsley and add the finely grated zest of 1 lemon plus 1 tablespoon lemon juice.

Herb butter: Substitute ½ teaspoon chopped lemon thyme, 2 teaspoons chopped chives and 1 teaspoon chopped rosemary for all but 2 teaspoons of the chopped parsley.

Tarragon butter: Substitute chopped tarragon for the parsley. If using the true French tarragon, add the full 2 tablespoons, but use a little less coarse tarragon.

Curry butter: Blend 1–2 teaspoons curry paste or powder with the butter at stage 1. The parsley could be omitted and 1 tablespoon smooth chutney substituted.

Savoury grilled chicken

you will need for 4 servings:
METRIC/IMPERIAL

1 shallot or small onion	salt and pepper
25 g/1 oz mushrooms	4 joints chicken
50 g/2 oz butter	2 tablespoons soft breadcrumbs
1 tablespoon chopped parsley	

1 Peel and finely chop the shallot or onion and chop the mushrooms.
2 Cream the butter with the chopped shallot or onion and add mushrooms, parsley and seasoning.
3 Spread the savoury butter mixture over the chicken joints and grill for 5 minutes.
4 Reduce the heat and sprinkle on the breadcrumbs. Cook until tender and serve with fried crumbs, grilled bacon and watercress.

Variations:
Mustard chicken: Omit the mushrooms and add 1 tablespoon made French or English mustard at stage 2.

Moroccan chicken

you will need for 4–6 servings:
METRIC/IMPERIAL

2 medium onions	pinch powdered saffron
2 cloves garlic	½ teaspoon ground cumin
¼ teaspoon ground coriander	3 tablespoons oil
3 tablespoons chopped mint	1 teaspoon paprika
	salt and pepper
	4–6 joints chicken

1 Peel and chop the onions and garlic very finely then crush, blend with all the other ingredients except the chicken and sieve or liquidise.
2 Rub the chicken with this mixture on both sides, pressing it in firmly. (The chicken joints will absorb the mixture better if skinned first.)
3 Grill until tender, turning once or twice and adding more of the onion mixture if any is left.
4 Serve with boiled rice; any onion mixture that may have dropped into the grill pan can be spooned over the chicken.

Chicken kebabs

you will need for 4 servings:

METRIC/IMPERIAL

1 small young frying chicken	25–50 g/1–2 oz melted butter, chicken fat or oil
4 rashers bacon	
few small button mushrooms	salt and pepper
	few tiny tomatoes

1 Cut the meat from the chicken in as thick pieces as possible. Divide into neat cubes.
2 Cut each rasher of bacon into 2–4 pieces, depending on length, and form into bacon rolls.
3 Arrange chicken, bacon rolls and mushrooms on long metal skewers. Brush with melted butter, fat or oil and season lightly.
4 Cook under a hot grill, turning frequently, or on a spit until the chicken is tender, about 10–15 minutes.
5 Put the tomatoes on the skewers for the last few minutes of cooking time. Serve with vegetables or boiled rice and a tomato, barbecue or sweet and sour sauce (see pages 43 and 34).

Variations:

Sour-sweet kebabs: Make a marinade (see page 30) and marinate the diced chicken for 1 hour then drain and put on metal skewers. Grill the chicken by itself or add bacon rolls, canned pineapple cubes, cooked prunes or small pickled or boiled onions to the skewers. Baste with the marinade instead of butter or other fat.

With pineapple and garlic balls: Add canned pineapple cubes to the skewers with the chicken and bacon rolls at stage 3. Prepare garlic balls (see page 29), place in the grill pan with a little melted butter then cook with the kebabs.

Curried chicken kebabs

you will need for 4 servings:

METRIC/IMPERIAL

1 teaspoon curry powder	oil or butter
1 teaspoon sugar	4 rashers streaky bacon
1 teaspoon cornflour	12 cooked prunes
2 tablespoons vinegar	salt and pepper
450 g/1 lb diced chicken	

1 Mix the curry powder, sugar, cornflour and vinegar together.
2 Brush the chicken with the oil or butter and dip in the cornflour mixture.
3 Cut each rasher of bacon into 2 or 3 pieces and form into bacon rolls; drain the prunes.
4 Skewer the pieces of chicken with the bacon and prunes alternately and season lightly.
5 Cook under a hot grill, turning frequently, or on a spit until chicken is tender.

Variation:

Saffron chicken kebabs: Substitute 1 teaspoon powdered saffron for the curry powder. The prunes can be omitted.

Chicken with apricots

you will need for 4 servings:

METRIC/IMPERIAL

4 joints chicken	1 tablespoon lemon juice
1 (213 g/7½ oz) can apricot halves	1 teaspoon chopped parsley
1 tablespoon oil	lemon slices (optional)
salt and pepper	

to garnish:
lemon wedges	watercress

1 Skin the chicken joints; drain the syrup from the apricots and pour it into a dish with the oil, seasoning and lemon juice. Add chopped parsley and lemon slices if used, then put the chicken joints into the marinade and leave for 1 hour, turning twice.
2 Lift the chicken out of the marinade and cook under a hot grill, turning several times and basting with the apricot mixture.
3 Add the apricots to the grill pan towards the end of the cooking period so that they can become hot.
4 Serve the chicken garnished with the apricots, wedges of lemon and watercress.

Variation:

Chicken with pineapple: Use canned pineapple rings instead of halved apricots. The pineapple rings can be sprinkled with sugar and glazed under the grill.

Devilled chicken with prunes

you will need for 4 servings:

METRIC/IMPERIAL
for devilled sauce:

2 large tomatoes	1 teaspoon tarragon vinegar
150 ml/¼ pint strong chicken stock	1 teaspoon chopped onion
1 tablespoon Worcestershire sauce	1 thin slice lemon
1 tablespoon mushroom ketchup	½ bay leaf
	salt and pepper
	175–225 g/6–8 oz cooked or canned prunes
4 joints chicken	1 tablespoon oil

to garnish:
watercress

1 First prepare the sauce: skin and finely chop the tomatoes and put into a pan with the rest of the ingredients, including the prunes.
2 Simmer without covering the pan until the sauce thickens slightly.
3 Brush the chicken with oil and cook under a pre-heated grill until brown on both sides.
4 Lift the prunes out of the sauce and put on to a hot serving dish.
5 Brush or spoon a little of the sauce over the chicken and continue cooking under the grill until tender.
6 Arrange the chicken joints on the serving dish and top with the rest of the sauce; garnish with water-cress. Serve with boiled rice.

Note:
The sauce can be sieved before using at stage 5.

Grilled chicken for slimmers

Grilling is ideal for dieters, for very little fat in the form of butter or oil is used. If, however, you have to omit all fats from your diet, choose very young tender chicken, so the cooking time is cut to a minimum. The spatchcock of chicken (see page 29) is particularly suitable.
Instead of using rich basting sauces or butter etc., flavour the chicken with tomato juice, orange juice or low-fat yogurt. Spread over the chicken or soak the chicken in it for about 15 minutes, then drain and grill in the usual way, basting with more of the juice or yogurt.

Viennese chicken

serves 4
Marinate 4 chicken joints in equal quantities of French dressing (see page 80) and apple or other fruit juice, season well and grill as usual. Add bacon rashers towards the end of the cooking time.

Barbecued chicken

Cooking over a barbecue is an ideal way of serving food. Chicken joints are excellent for this; you can also barbecue whole birds, but these must be young and tender.

Stews and sauces can be cooked over the fire, but make sure you have strong, heavy pans.
Arrange the bricks and top with one of your oven shelves. If you intend to cook whole chickens, build the bricks high enough so the bird is not too near the fierce heat.
To test the heat: wait until the charcoal glows red (this will take about an hour). If your barbecue is heated by electricity or gas, the manufacturers' instructions will cover heating time. Always keep children away from the fire.
Many stores sell ready barbecued chickens, already cooked. Reheat for a very short time over the barbecue fire, basting with your chosen sauce.
While you can freeze the cooked chicken to reheat, it is better to cook the bird when it is required. Frozen chickens can be used (but note the comments on defrosting under grilled chickens, page 29, and roast chickens, page 35).
The various highly-flavoured marinades and barbecue sauces can be frozen for a limited period, i.e. 2–3 weeks, but lose their flavour with prolonged storage.

Orange ginger sauce

you will need for 4 servings:

METRIC/IMPERIAL	
4–5 gingernut biscuits	2 tablespoons white
150 ml/¼ pint canned	vinegar
orange juice	salt and pepper
50–75 g/2–3 oz seedless	50 g/2 oz brown sugar
raisins	1 tablespoon oil

1 Crush the biscuits and blend with all the other ingredients in a saucepan, then heat until the crumbs are softened.
2 If using for a basting sauce, omit the raisins.

Variation:
Orange cranberry sauce: Omit the biscuits to make a thinner sauce, and add 75–100 g/3–4 oz cranberries. You may need a little more sugar.

Raisin sauce

This is better served with plain barbecued chicken, rather than as a basting sauce.

you will need for 4 servings:

METRIC/IMPERIAL	
1 tablespoon cornflour	salt and pepper
300 ml/½ pint chicken	2 teaspoons dry mustard
stock or water	1–2 tablespoons brown
100 g/4 oz seedless	sugar
raisins	25 g/1 oz butter
2 tablespoons vinegar	

1 Blend the cornflour with a little of the stock or

water, pour with the rest of the stock into a saucepan and add the rest of the ingredients.

2 Stir over the heat until the sauce thickens slightly.

Note:
As it is not very comfortable to stir over the heat of the barbecue, you may prefer to make the sauce in the kitchen and reheat as required.

Sour cream and cucumber sauce

serves 4–6

Blend 300 ml/½ pint soured cream (or yogurt) with 2 tablespoons white vinegar, ½–1 tablespoon castor sugar, seasoning and a generous pinch of dry mustard. Cut half a large cucumber into matchstick pieces (peel if wished) and blend with the mixture.

Tangy barbecue sauce

you will need for 4 servings:

METRIC/IMPERIAL	
½ small onion	2 tablespoons wine
I clove garlic	vinegar
I sprig parsley	2 tablespoons oil
150 ml/¼ pint tomato	I teaspoon
ketchup	Worcestershire sauce
	pepper to taste

1 Peel and chop or mince onion, garlic and parsley and put into a large screw top jar with the other ingredients. Cover and shake vigorously until all ingredients are well blended.

2 Leave to stand for 24 hours, shaking occasionally.

Accompaniments

One of the best accompaniments to hot barbecued chicken is a salad. While you can cook vegetables in pans over the fire, this means the bother of straining and it is easier to cook vegetables in foil as below.

Jacket potatoes: Scrub the potatoes, prick with a fork and wrap in a double thickness of foil. Allow 1 hour for medium old or smaller new potatoes and up to 1½ hours for large ones over the barbecue fire. When cooked, split and top with butter, soured cream, cream cheese or yogurt and chopped parsley or chives (keep these in a polythene container until ready to serve). When you are cooking potatoes at

home in the oven there is no need to wrap them in foil. Prepare as above and bake in a moderate oven (180°C, 350°F, Gas Mark 4).

Barbecued carrots, etc.: Scrub, peel and slice carrots and put in foil with a knob of butter and seasoning. Wrap firmly. Allow about 1¼ hours over the barbecue fire. Other root vegetables take the same amount of time. Mushrooms can be cooked like this as well; they will take about 15 minutes. Shelled peas need a little water added to the butter and seasoning; omit water when cooking frozen peas this way. Allow 10–15 minutes.

Barbecued tomatoes: Halve, season well, top with butter and cook on open foil over the barbecue fire for about 10 minutes.

Barbecued chicken joints

Lay the joints on oiled foil over the barbecue and brush with melted fat, butter, oil or one of the basting sauces or marinades. Cook for 15–20 minutes, turning and basting several times. Any of the recipes for grilled chicken (see pages 29–30) are suitable.

Barbecued whole chickens

Allow the same time as for quick roasting (see page 36). If you put stuffing into the bird, calculate the weight with the stuffing. Baste the chicken well during cooking. The whole bird can be put on foil or to stand on the bars above the fire.

Garlic chicken legs

Sometimes a recipe calls for chicken breasts and this may leave you with legs of chicken. The following recipes are excellent ways of cooking these over the barbecue. The legs could be cooked under a hot grill instead if wished.

you will need for 4 servings:

METRIC/IMPERIAL
4 legs of young chicken

for the marinade:

2 cloves garlic	2 tablespoons tomato
salt and pepper	ketchup
3 tablespoons oil	2 teaspoons
2 tablespoons vinegar	Worcestershire sauce

1 Make slits in the chicken flesh (to allow the marinade

flavour to penetrate thoroughly); peel and crush the garlic.

2 Mix all the marinade ingredients with the garlic, then place the chicken in this mixture for an hour, turning once or twice. Drain and cook over the barbecue, basting with the mixture once or twice.

Crispy chicken

serves 4

Brush 4 chicken joints (the legs are always easiest to eat with your fingers) with oil or melted butter, sprinkle with seasoning and barbecue until nearly tender; turn and baste during cooking. Have ready one of the following toppings. Spread the topping over one side of the chicken only, place this side down on the foil and cook for a few minutes only over the bars of the barbecue fire. Serve with a sauce.

Cheese topping: Cream 40 g/1½ oz butter or margarine with seasoning and a generous pinch of celery salt and dry mustard. Add 50 g/2 oz dried breadcrumbs and 50 g/2 oz grated cheese.

Cornflake topping: Cream 40 g/1½ oz butter or margarine with 1 teaspoon finely grated lemon rind, salt and pepper. Add 100 g/4 oz coarsely crushed cornflakes.

Potato topping: Cream 40 g/1½ oz butter or margarine with 1 teaspoon made mustard. Add 100 g/ 4 oz crushed potato crisps.

Sweet-sour topping: Blend 50 g/2 oz butter or margarine with 2 tablespoons sweet chutney, 2 teaspoons vinegar and 100 g/4 oz soft breadcrumbs.

Variation:

Sausage surprise: Bone each uncooked chicken portion and coat in sausagemeat (allow about 100 g/ 4 oz sausagemeat to each young chicken joint). Cook steadily over the barbecue until sausagemeat and chicken are cooked (20–25 minutes); turn frequently. Cooked chicken pieces could be coated in the same way. Baste with a sauce during cooking.

Roast Chicken

Roasting chicken is one of the most delicious ways of cooking a bird, and the following method will ensure perfect results. Frozen birds must be *completely* defrosted before roasting.

Always put fat of some kind over the chicken, since the breast is lean and will dry. You can roast chicken wrapped in foil, in a modern polythene roasting bag, in a covered roasting tin or in an uncovered dish.

Take care not to overcook the bird. Times for roasting are given, but while this is a very good guide sometimes a bird takes a *little* longer because it is particularly thick on the breast or legs for its weight. On the other hand, a bird that has fairly big bones and a small amount of flesh could take 5–10 minutes less cooking time, so test carefully. Remember that the weight of stuffing must be included in determining the total cooking time.

If you are roasting a large bird it is wise to place the breast side down for the first half of the roasting time; this keeps it appreciably moister.

If roasting the bird in an open tin, it is wise to baste with the hot fat; do this once or twice for a small bird, three times for a larger bird. If, however, you cook the bird with the breast down, basting need be done only once when the bird is placed breast up to brown.

A covered roasting tin gives a certain amount of basting during cooking, as the fat splashes up to the top of the tin then drops on to the breast of the chicken. This means the skin will brown but may not become crisp, so remove the lid for the last 15 minutes of cooking time. It takes a little longer for heat to penetrate a covered tin, so allow an extra 5–10 minutes of cooking time.

Using foil or roasting bags

Foil has the great advantage of keeping the bird very moist, but does not allow it to crisp. The bird can be brushed with oil, melted fat or butter, then wrapped completely in foil. If this method is used, allow at least 15 minutes extra cooking time. Unwrap the bird or remove the foil for the last 15 minutes to allow it to crisp and brown.

You must buy the special roasting bags, as ordinary polythene bags are unsuitable. Prepare the chicken, cover with butter or fat, place in the bag and seal; roast as usual. The bird browns well, but if you want a really crisp skin remove from the bag about 20 minutes before the end of the cooking period.

Very slow roasting

Very slow roasting is recommended for tenderising old boiling fowls but could be used for other younger birds if more convenient. The fowl can be cooked in an open or covered roasting tin to allow the generous amount of fat generally found on older birds to run into the tin, or it could be loosely covered with foil. If you wrap the bird completely in foil, allow 15–20 minutes extra cooking time and open the foil for the last 30–45 minutes.

Roast in a very cool oven (120°C, 250°F, Gas Mark ½) for 2 hours for the first half kilo/1 lb plus an extra 35 minutes for each extra half kilo/1 lb.

Roasting boiling fowls

To boil a boiling fowl and achieve the appearance of a roast chicken, you could boil or preferably steam the fowl for two-thirds of the recommended time (see page 17), then lift the bird out of the stock or steamer and pat dry with kitchen paper.

Put into hot fat and roast for the rest of the cooking time. Roast slowly for a further 1–1½ hours.

If you are in doubt as to the tenderness of the boiling fowl it is better to steam or boil it for the total cooking time. lift out and dry, then brown in hot fat for about 20 minutes in a hot oven (220°C, 425°F, Gas Mark 7).

Quick roasting

The quick method of roasting is suitable for fresh young roasting chickens or capons. Prepare the bird then weigh.

Roast in a moderately hot to hot oven (200–220°C, 400–425°F, Gas Mark 6–7). After about 45 minutes the heat can be *slightly* reduced if the bird is browning too quickly. Cook for 15 minutes per half kilo/per lb plus 15 minutes extra for the *trussed* weight and including stuffing.

Slow roasting

You may prefer to roast young birds more slowly, in which case cook in a moderate oven (160–180°C, 325–350°F, Gas Mark 3–4) for 25 minutes per half kilo/per lb to 2·75 kg/6 lb plus 25 minutes extra. For chickens over this weight allow 20 minutes for each additional half kilo/1 lb.

This method is better for defrosted frozen birds but is also suitable for fresh birds, although I personally prefer the quicker roasting for prime poultry.

To test if chicken is cooked, insert the tip of a knife between the leg and body; if any red juice flows the bird is undercooked.

Using a spit

Many modern cookers have a rotisserie attachment which is an ideal way to cook whole young roasting chickens or joints of frying chicken or young turkey. Carefully follow the operating and maintenance directions issued for your equipment and keep it scrupulously clean. Make sure the spit will turn evenly and that you fix the chicken securely.

Cook a whole chicken on a spit placed under the grill for 25 minutes per half kilo/per lb plus 25 minutes extra. Baste the chicken with melted butter, dripping or other fat or oil during cooking.

If the spit is situated in the oven then cook in a moderately hot to hot oven (200–220°C, 400–425°F, Gas Mark 6–7) and allow 15 minutes per half kilo/ per lb plus 15 minutes extra.

The advantage of spit cooking is that the birds brown evenly, but they must be basted thoroughly to prevent the breast flesh from drying out. Always put a tin under the spit to catch the surplus fat.If the spit is in the oven and a fairly high temperature used,

potatoes can be roasted at the same time in the tin under the spit.

If cooking a number of chickens for a special occasion, try to buy birds of the same weight, to ensure they are evenly roasted. Frozen whole chickens must be defrosted before cooking.

Chicken joints will take approximately the same time as grilled chicken (see page 29). Turkey joints will take the same time as whole chicken.

To give flavour when spit roasting, season the birds or use the suggestions under barbecued chicken (see pages 33 and 34).

Roasting a boned chicken

A boned chicken is so easy to carve that it makes it worthwhile roasting one, especially if you want to serve the bird for a party. Follow the directions for boning (see page 7). You then will have a flat piece of meat. Choose a stuffing (see pages 44–46) or flavour as for roast chicken.

Spread the stuffing over the flesh, form into a neat shape and tie. Spread butter or fat over the bird and roast a fresh bird in a moderately hot to hot oven (200–220°C, 400–425°F, Gas Mark 6–7) for 15 minutes per half kilo/per lb plus 15 minutes extra, and a defrosted frozen bird in a moderate oven (160–180°C, 325–350°F, Gas Mark 3–4) for 25 minutes per half kilo/per lb plus 25 minutes extra. Since the flesh is very solid, I find it better to add about one-third extra cooking time on to these amounts.

Roasting spring chickens

Small spring chickens can be stuffed or roasted without a stuffing. Cover with plenty of butter or fat during cooking as there is no fat on the flesh, and put a knob of butter inside to keep the birds moist. Cream cheese and skinned de-seeded grapes can be placed inside the birds if liked.

Freezing roast chicken

As stated before, it is essential to defrost an uncooked frozen bird before roasting it. If you want to roast, then freeze the bird, it is a good idea to joint it after cooking to make defrosting easier. If you carve the cooked bird into thin slices before freezing it tends to be flavourless when thawed out.

Using turkey portions

All the recipes for roast chicken can be adapted for turkey portions, often sold in the supermarket. Place the cut side of the turkey portion down. Any stuffing can be pressed against it, or cooked in a separate dish. Timing for cooking may be a little shorter than for chicken, since the portions are fairly shallow and the heat penetrates more easily.

Flavourings for roast chicken

Stuffing and sauces give interest and flavour to chicken, but the following are quick and simple alternatives.

Butter: Put a knob of well seasoned butter inside the bird and brush the outside with more seasoned butter.

Cheese: Put 75–100 g/3–4 oz cream cheese into the bird before cooking. Alternatively spread the cream cheese or sprinkle 50 g/2 oz grated cheese over the bird 10 minutes before the end of the cooking time and return to the oven.

Cream: Pour off the surplus fat from the tin about 10 minutes before the end of the cooking time. Coat the chicken with a little well seasoned double cream or soured cream and continue cooking.

Garlic: Peel 1–2 cloves of garlic and cut into thin slivers. Insert these under the skin of the bird before coating with fat.

Honey: Brush 1–2 tablespoons honey or honey blended with 1 tablespoon lemon juice over the chicken 10 minutes before the end of the cooking time and return to the oven.

Lemon: Put segments of lemon inside the bird and squeeze lemon juice over the bird after coating with butter or fat.

Onions: Put several peeled onions inside the bird before cooking.

Potatoes: Put several peeled potatoes inside the bird before cooking.

Redcurrant jelly: Melt 2–3 tablespoons redcurrant jelly. Brush over the chicken 10 minutes before the end of the cooking time and return to the oven.

Rosemary: Put a sprig of fresh rosemary inside the bird. Brush the bird with melted butter blended with ½–1 teaspoon chopped fresh rosemary. Other herbs (tarragon or chives) could be used instead.

Country-style roast chicken: Add whole onions, cored but unpeeled apples (choose the dessert type that cook well) to the tin, turn in the hot fat and cook with the bird. Add a little cider to the gravy.

Roast chicken with fruit: About 15 minutes before the end of the cooking time pour off any surplus fat. Add the contents of a medium can of fruit or the equivalent in cooked fruit with the syrup; the most suitable are apricots, peaches, pineapple or prunes. Stir the liquid into the fat in the pan then continue cooking the bird. Lift the bird and fruit on to a serving dish, then thicken the liquid for gravy.

Accompaniments for roast chicken

A large roasting chicken is generally stuffed (see pages 44–46). Spring chicken can be stuffed or cooked without stuffing and served with the same accompaniments, either bread or cranberry sauce (see pages 43), fried crumbs, game chips, bacon rolls, forcemeat balls and/or cooked sausages. The sausages can either be put into the roasting tin round the chicken 30–40 minutes before the end of the cooking time, or cooked separately. Roast potatoes or any other vegetables can be served with the roast chicken, and a thickened gravy is usually served if the bird is stuffed.
To keep spring chickens moist without using stuffing, put a knob of butter inside each bird before cooking and take care not to overcook the chicken.

Fried crumbs: Make large crumbs from bread and fry in butter until crisp and golden brown; drain on absorbent paper. This can be done in advance and the crumbs reheated gently in the oven before serving.

Bacon rolls: Remove the rinds from rashers of streaky bacon and halve the rashers. Stretch the bacon with the back of a knife (this makes the bacon roll more easily). Form into rolls and put on metal skewers. Either put round the chicken towards the end of the cooking period or grill or fry separately.

Forcemeat balls: Chop 2 rashers of bacon finely. Mix with 100 g/4 oz soft breadcrumbs, 50 g/2 oz shredded suet, 1–1½ tablespoons chopped parsley, 1 teaspoon chopped or ½ teaspoon dried mixed herbs, the grated rind of 1 lemon, seasoning to taste and 1 egg. Form into balls. Roast round the chicken or in a greased tin for the last 30 minutes of the cooking time. Serves 4.

Game chips: Peel then slice potatoes very thinly. Dry well in a tea towel or on absorbent paper. Fry in very hot oil or fat until crisp and golden brown. Drain on absorbent paper. These can be fried in advance then reheated on a flat plate or dish in the oven.

Roast potatoes: Peel potatoes then roast in hot fat round the chicken or in fat in a separate tin. Allow about 50 minutes–1 hour for medium potatoes at the same temperature as for the quick method of roasting (see page 36). If you like a 'floury' taste to roast potatoes, cook the potatoes for about 15 minutes in boiling salted water, drain and pat dry then continue cooking in hot fat.

Macedoine of vegetables: This is used as a garnish for some chicken dishes. Peel then dice root vegetables (potatoes, carrots, turnips, swedes), add shelled peas and chopped green beans then cook in boiling salted water until soft. Drain and toss in hot butter.

Gravy for roast chicken

you will need for 4 servings:

METRIC/IMPERIAL

giblets	fat
salt and pepper	25 g/1 oz flour
water	

1 Simmer the giblets of the bird with seasoning in just enough water to cover.
2 Allow about 1 hour in a covered pan or 20–25 minutes in a pressure cooker at High (15 lb) pressure. When tender, strain off stock.
3 When bird is roasted lift on to a hot dish. Pour off any surplus fat, but leave approximately 1 tablespoon and any residue of stuffing in the tin.
4 Stir in the flour and cook gently until golden brown.
5 Gradually blend in 450–600 ml/¾–1 pint giblet stock. Bring to the boil and cook until thickened; strain and reheat. A tablespoon of sherry or port wine can be added.

Variations:

Thick gravy: Add only 300–450 ml/½–¾ pint stock at stage 5.

Flavoured gravy: Use part red or white wine instead of all stock at stage 5. Use the water from cooking green vegetables, thus retaining the mineral salts. Add a little cream just before serving.

Sauce poulette: Fry a chopped onion and 2–3 chopped mushrooms in the fat in the tin at stage 3; stir in 1 tablespoon sherry and 2 tablespoons double cream just before serving.

Using chicken dripping
When you have finished roasting a chicken you generally pour the surplus fat away, leaving just enough for the gravy. Never waste this fat. Pour it into a basin and you will find that when it has solidified it gives you a layer of deliciously flavoured dripping and possibly a thick golden brown jelly underneath.
This jelly can be added to sauces and gravies to produce a very rich flavour. It is also ideal to use in place of some of the water for an aspic jelly (see page 19).

To glaze a chicken
The jelly described above can be melted, then cooled and allowed to stiffen slightly and brushed over a chicken to glaze.

Pot roast chicken

you will need for 4–8 servings:

METRIC/IMPERIAL

50 g/2 oz fat	225 g/8 oz carrots
1 roasting chicken	225 g/8 oz small onions
300 ml/½ pint stock or water	salt and pepper

1 Heat the fat in a large saucepan and turn the chicken in it until golden brown, then lift out and put to one side.
2 Put in the stock or water with the peeled vegetables, which should be left whole.
3 Put the chicken on top, adding seasoning, and cover with a very tight-fitting lid. If you are not satisfied with the lid of the pan, put paper or foil underneath.
4 Turn the heat down to low and cook for approximately 15 minutes per half kilo/per lb of chicken and 15 minutes over; the liquid should simmer throughout the cooking time.

Note:
The chicken will not be very crisp, but it does taste like roast chicken as it is not immersed in the liquid. You could put the chicken on a trivet in place of the vegetables.

Pot roasting in a pressure cooker

You can use the same ingredients as in the pot roast above, or substitute other vegetables. Choose a young chicken not exceeding 1·5 kg/3 lb in weight.

1 Put a little fat into the base of the pressure cooker and brown the chicken in this, turning it over several times.
2 Remove the chicken from the pan; brown potatoes. onions etc., if you would like them coloured; they will not be crisp, since liquid is added to the pan. Remove the vegetables and put to one side. Pour off any surplus fat; this is important if the gravy is not to be too greasy.
3 Add 450 ml/¾ pint liquid (water, chicken stock or stock and wine) and heat it in the open pan, stirring well to absorb any fat left in the pan; this will give an excellent gravy. The giblets could be added if wished.
4 Place the browned chicken in the pressure cooker on the trivet. Fix the lid, bring rapidly to High (15 lb) pressure and lower the heat. Allow 5 minutes per half kilo/per lb.
5 Reduce pressure under cold water 5–6 minutes before the end of the cooking time, remove the lid and add the browned vegetables; re-fix the lid, bring once again to pressure and continue cooking.
6 Reduce the pressure under cold water, remove lid and lift the chicken and vegetables out on to a dish. Remove the trivet (plus giblets) and thicken the gravy in the open pan.

Chicken Strasbourg

you will need for 4 servings:

METRIC/IMPERIAL

1 roasting chicken	25–50 g/1–2 oz butter
225 g/8 oz pâté	salt and pepper

1 Stuff the breast of the chicken with the pâté by

making a pocket in the uncooked flesh. Melt the butter and brush over the chicken, seasoning lightly.
2 Wrap the chicken in foil or put into a roasting bag, then cook as table for roasting (see page 35) or steam over a pan of boiling water, allowing 15 minutes per half kilo/per lb and 15 minutes over.
3 Do not unwrap the foil, but allow to cool first. Remove the foil. Serve cold with salads.

Note:
This is a recipe in which one could benefit from boning before cooking the chicken (see page 7).

Variation:
Use cream cheese flavoured with chopped canned red pepper and chopped lemon thyme instead of pâté.

Roast chicken Espagnole

you will need for 4 servings:
METRIC/IMPERIAL

1 roasting chicken	rich or economical Espagnole sauce (see page 42)

to garnish:
macedoine of vegetables
   (see page 37)

1 Roast the chicken according to its weight (see page 35).
2 Slice or joint the bird, depending on its size.
3 Serve with Espagnole sauce and garnish with the cooked vegetables.

Variations:
Roast chicken with peppers: When the chicken is nearly cooked pour off all but 2 tablespoons fat. Add 2–3 sliced red and/or green peppers, discarding the cores and seeds, plus 2 cloves peeled and crushed garlic, and continue cooking. Serve with Espagnole sauce.

Roast chicken Lyonnaise: Brown the chicken in the hot fat, lift from the roasting tin and add thinly sliced onions and potatoes. Season well, replace the chicken and continue cooking. Serve with gravy or Espagnole sauce.

Salmis of chicken

you will need for 6–8 servings:
METRIC/IMPERIAL

1 roasting chicken	few sprigs of parsley
1 carrot	1 sprig of thyme
2 shallots	1 blade of mace
100 g/4 oz lean ham	25 g/1 oz flour
50 g/2 oz small mush-rooms	600 ml/1 pint chicken stock
50 g/2 oz butter	150 ml/¼ pint dry sherry
1 bay leaf	

1 Roast the chicken (see page 35), cool, skin and cut into neat joints.
2 Peel and dice the carrot and shallots, and dice the ham, leaving the mushrooms whole.
3 Heat the butter and add the carrot, shallots, herbs and mace; stir in the flour and fry until browned then add the stock and sherry.
4 Add the skin from the chicken and simmer until the liquid is reduced by half. Strain then bring it to the boil again; add the ham, mushrooms and chicken pieces and reheat.
5 Serve with fried sippets of bread, crusty French bread or jacket potatoes.

Variation:
Salmis of chicken with chestnuts: Omit the mushrooms and carrot in the recipe above and add about 225 g/8 oz peeled chestnuts at stage 4 with the chicken. The chicken could also be filled with a chestnut stuffing (see page 44) before roasting.

Note:
A salmis is a good way of reheating a ready-cooked chicken. If you would rather re-roast it, spread the bird with plenty of butter, wrap in foil or put into a roasting bag and allow 7 minutes per half kilo/per lb in a moderate oven (160°C, 325°F, Gas Mark 3).

Steamed chicken

All types of chicken can be cooked by steaming. It is a particularly good method if you want the flesh kept fairly firm and dry to use in recipes. The liquid under the steamer absorbs very little flavour from the bird so is of no value as stock.

The usual way to steam is to put the bird into a steamer over a pan of boiling water. If cooking a boiling fowl and it is fat, it needs seasoning only. If, on the other hand, it is quite a lean bird it is a good idea to either brush with a little melted butter, wrap in buttered paper or foil, or place in a roasting bag.

Do not cook the bird too quickly. The water in the saucepan should boil steadily; as the bird is not in direct contact with the liquid it needs just a little more cooking time than when boiling, i.e. allow nearly 20 minutes per half kilo/per lb and 20 minutes extra for young birds (for complete timings see under boiling, page 17). The giblets may either be steamed round the chicken or cooked in the water under the steamer, in which case they will add flavour to the liquid.

Freezing steamed chicken
The comments on freezing other types of cooked chicken apply to chicken after it has been steamed.

If you have to pre-cook, then freeze, the bird will lose quite a lot of flavour. Joint, rather than carve, the chicken. If you need to carve slices, keep them fairly thick and layer with pieces of waxed or grease-proof paper, so they may easily be separated.

Steamed chicken for slimmers
Steaming is an ideal way of cooking a chicken if you are on a diet, for it retains rather more taste than when boiled. If you are on a low-fat diet, remove the skin after cooking. You can add flavour to the bird as it steams if you put herbs – rosemary, parsley, lemon thyme or garlic – inside or sprinkle them on the flesh. Rubbing the flesh with seasoned lemon juice or tomato juice before steaming gives a very pleasant flavour as well.

Chicken niçoise

serves 4–6
Joint the chicken. Cut a large square of foil for each chicken joint. Skin and slice a tomato and place a couple of slices on the foil. Add the well seasoned chicken joint, chopped chives, and cover with more skinned sliced tomato plus a little grated onion if desired. Wrap up the foil to make a parcel and steam for 1½ hours for an older fowl or about 45–50 minutes for younger chicken. Vary with sliced mushrooms or add a little wine to the parcel.

Chaudfroid of chicken (2)

This is one of the most attractive ways to prepare a whole cold chicken to serve for a party. The chicken can be boiled and coated, but the chicken is firmer in texture if it is steamed. The recipe below gives the classic version of this sauce. Steam the chicken, remove the skin while the bird is warm, cool and coat as below.

to coat a chicken of about 2·25 kg/5 lb you will need:
METRIC/IMPERIAL

600 ml/1 pint Allemande, béchamel or velouté sauce (see pages 41 and 42)	600 ml/1 pint aspic jelly (either use packet or see page 19)
	1 teaspoon gelatine
	garnishes

1 Make the chosen sauce.
2 Prepare the jelly (this should be done ahead if you are making your own); put a little aside in a separate container. Dissolve the gelatine in the hot jelly (see page 14).
3 Blend the sauce and jelly together and allow the chaudfroid to become cold and slightly set, until it is the consistency of a syrup. The small amount of jelly set aside should be kept liquid. Keep the chaudfroid sauce covered as it cools so that a skin does not form.
4 Stand the chicken on a wire cooling tray with a dish underneath to catch drips. Brush or spread a thin layer of sauce over the chicken, allow to stiffen slightly then repeat with a second layer.
5 Prepare the garnishes: choose small diamond-shaped pieces from a selection of canned red pepper, truffle or mushroom, gherkin, etc. Dip into the reserved aspic jelly and place in position. When firm, serve with salad.

Sauces and Stuffings

Sauces

Chicken can be blended with a variety of sauces, ranging from the delicate taste of a white sauce to the full flavour of a curry or Espagnole sauce. Some of the basic sauces are given below, others as part of a complete recipe.

To make good sauces

1 Always allow sufficient cooking time when flour or cornflour are used in the sauce; this makes certain you have a smooth texture and no flavour of un-cooked flour.
2 It is better to be slightly generous with the amount of liquid in the recipe so that the sauce thickens by evaporation.
3 By adding some chicken stock to the basic sauce you get a related flavour to the main dish.
4 If the sauce appears slightly lumpy, whisk sharply or liquidise. If you use the latter method, which gives a velvet smooth texture, the sauce will be thinner and you should thicken by evaporation.
5 When egg yolks and/or lemon juice or wine are added to a sauce, care should be taken that the sauce does not boil, but simmers gently; stir during this process. This is to prevent curdling.
6 To keep a cooked sauce waiting: cover the top with damp paper, a little extra butter or other fat, or a layer of cold liquid. This prevents a skin forming. Whisk as the sauce is reheated.

Freezing sauces
Some sauces may separate or become thin when frozen. It is less likely if you substitute cornflour for flour, i.e. 15 g/½ oz cornflour instead of 25 g/1 oz flour, or use potato flour (same quantity as ordinary flour).
If the sauce is thin add extra thickening when re-heating; whisk well for a smooth texture. Try to avoid adding egg yolks, wine or cream before freezing the sauce.

White sauce

This is a basic sauce that can be served as it is with boiled or steamed poultry. The sauce can be made more interesting by the variations which follow.

you will need for 4 servings:
METRIC/IMPERIAL

25 g/1 oz butter or margarine	300 ml/½ pint milk for coating consistency or
25 g/1 oz flour	600 ml/1 pint milk for
150 ml/¼ pint milk for panada (very thick binding consistency) or	thin white sauce (for soups)
	salt and pepper

1 Heat butter or margarine gently. Remove from the heat and stir in the flour.
2 Return to the heat and cook gently for a few minutes, so that the roux (as the mixture is called) does not brown.
3 Again remove the pan from the heat and gradually blend in the desired amount of cold milk.
4 Bring to the boil and cook, stirring with a wooden spoon, until thickened and smooth; season to taste.

Note:
The following sauces can be used as a basis for heating through diced or sliced cooked chicken or turkey to make a satisfying dish. In this case it would be advisable to use about 25% more liquid to allow for evaporation due to the longer heating period.

Variations:
Basic sauce for chicken: Use half chicken stock and half milk; chicken fat could be substituted for butter or margarine.

Allemande (German) sauce: Use all chicken stock and no milk. When the sauce has thickened whisk with an egg yolk, return to pan and simmer for several minutes; then whisk in an extra 25 g/1 oz butter and 1 tablespoon lemon juice.

Béchamel sauce: Infuse a piece of onion, carrot or celery in the warm milk or milk and stock; allow to stand for at least 30 minutes then strain and make up to full quantity required.

Caper sauce: Add 2 teaspoons bottled capers and a little of their vinegar to the thickened sauce. This is excellent with fried or grilled chicken.

Cheese sauce: Add 75–100 g/3–4 oz grated Cheddar or other cooking cheese to the white sauce after it has thickened. Do not overcook, but simply allow the cheese to melt.

Cream sauce: Use half milk and half chicken stock. When the sauce has thickened add several table-spoons double cream.

Giblet sauce: Add the neatly diced cooked giblet meat to the white sauce.

Hard-boiled egg sauce: Add 1–2 chopped hard-boiled eggs to the white or cream sauce.

Hot cucumber sauce: Simmer ½ peeled diced medium cucumber in 150 ml/¼ pint chicken stock until tender. Sieve or liquidise until it is a smooth purée. Add to the white sauce and heat gently. Tint lightly with a little green food colouring. Flavour with 2 tablespoons soured cream and reheat.

Liver sauce: Add the finely chopped cooked chicken liver to the white, béchamel or cream sauce.

Mornay sauce: Add 75–100 g/3–4 oz grated Gruyère or other cooking cheese to the béchamel sauce.

Mushroom sauce: Add 50–100 g/2–4 oz fried sliced mushrooms to the white or béchamel sauce.

Mustard sauce: Add 1–2 teaspoons dry mustard with the flour at stage 1 then proceed as for white or béchamel sauce. 1–2 tablespoons cream could also be stirred into the thickened sauce. This is particularly good with grilled chicken.

Onion sauce: Peel and dice 2 medium onions and simmer in 300 ml/½ pint chicken stock until tender. Use only 150 ml/¼ pint milk to make the white sauce then add the onion mixture and heat together.

Parsley sauce: Add 1–2 tablespoons chopped parsley to the white, béchamel or cream sauce. If the parsley is simmered in the sauce it will give a mellower flavour than if added at the last minute.

Velouté sauce: Use only chicken stock. A richer sauce can be made by using only 15 g/½ oz flour and blending 2 egg yolks, whisked with 2 tablespoons cream and a squeeze of lemon juice, into the thickened sauce.

Brown sauce

Brown sauce may not be served with chicken as often as other sauces but it is the basis for several interesting sauces which blend very well with poultry.

you will need for 4 servings:

METRIC/IMPERIAL	
25–50 g/1–2 oz butter, margarine or chicken fat	300 ml/½ pint well seasoned brown stock
1 small onion	for coating consistency
1 small carrot	1–2 tablespoons tomato
25 g/1 oz flour	purée (optional)

1 Melt the fat gently. Peel and chop the onion and carrot and fry in the fat until softened.
2 Remove from the heat and stir in the flour. Return to the heat and cook gently, then again remove from the heat and gradually add the stock.
3 Bring to the boil and cook, stirring with a wooden

spoon, until thickened. Add tomato purée if liked.
4 Strain or liquidise the sauce if a smooth texture is required.

Variations:

Port wine sauce: Substitute 3–4 tablespoons port wine for the same amount of stock. This is excellent with fried or grilled chicken.

Game sauce: Use only 150 ml/¼ pint stock and add 150 ml/¼ pint red wine, 1 tablespoon brown malt or red wine vinegar, 1–2 tablespoons sugar and 4 tablespoons redcurrant jelly. Stir until the jelly has dissolved. This can be served hot or cold, and is equally good with roasted chicken or turkey as a change from a gravy.

Economical Espagnole sauce

you will need for 4 servings:

METRIC/IMPERIAL	
1 large tomato	25 g/1 oz fat
2–3 mushrooms or equivalent in stalks	25 g/1 oz flour
	600 ml/1 pint brown or
1 onion	giblet stock
1 carrot	salt and pepper

1 Slice the tomato and mushrooms, or chop the stalks; peel and slice the onion and carrot.
2 Heat fat and stir in flour; cook for several minutes, stirring well, until brown.
3 Add the stock to the pan gradually. Bring to the boil, stirring until smooth, then add all the vegetables and season well.
4 Simmer in a covered pan for about 45 minutes until the sauce has thickened and the vegetables are very tender. Rub through a sieve or liquidise and reheat.

Variations:

Quick Espagnole sauce: Grate the onion and carrot at stage 1. Substitute 1 tablespoon tomato purée or ketchup for the tomato. The mushrooms or mushroom stalks should be very finely chopped, and there should be no need to sieve or liquidise.

Rich (classic) Espagnole sauce: Use 50 g/2 oz fat or butter and toss the vegetables in it before adding the flour. Increase the amount of mushrooms to 4 large ones and use 2 large tomatoes. Add 4 tablespoons sherry to the sieved or liquidised sauce.

Devilled sauce: Add 1–3 teaspoons made mustard, a generous pinch of cayenne pepper and up to 1 tablespoon Worcestershire sauce to the sieved or liquidised economical or rich Espagnole sauce.

Madeira sauce: Use half stock and half Madeira wine in the economical or rich Espagnole sauce.

Poivrade sauce: Add 6–12 peppercorns to the economical or rich Espagnole sauce at stage 3. Add brandy instead of sherry to the sieved or liquidised rich Espagnole sauce.

Bread sauce

you will need for 4–6 servings:
METRIC/IMPERIAL
1 small onion
2–3 cloves (optional)
300 ml/½ pint milk
50 g/2 oz soft
  breadcrumbs
25–50 g/1–2 oz butter or
  margarine
salt and pepper

1 Peel the onion and stick the cloves, if used, firmly into the onion.
2 Put the onion into the milk together with the other ingredients and slowly bring to the boil.
3 Remove from the heat and stand in a warm place for as long as possible.
4 Just before serving the meal, heat the sauce gently, beating with a wooden spoon. Remove onion before putting into a sauce boat.

Variations:
Add 1–2 tablespoons double cream or a generous pinch of mixed spice to the sauce.

Creamed curry sauce

you will need for 4 servings:
METRIC/IMPERIAL
50 g/2 oz butter or
  margarine
½–1 tablespoon curry
  powder
25 g/1 oz flour
300 ml/½ pint milk or
150 ml/¼ pint milk and
150 ml/¼ pint chicken
  stock for coating sauce
salt and pepper
pinch sugar

1 Heat the butter in a pan and stir in the curry powder and flour.
2 Cook gently for several minutes without allowing the mixture to brown. Gradually add the liquid, bring to the boil, stirring, and cook until thickened and smooth.
3 Season and sweeten to taste.

Tomato sauce

you will need for 4 servings:
METRIC/IMPERIAL
1 small onion
1 carrot
5 large fresh or canned
  tomatoes
1 rasher bacon
25 g/1 oz butter
1 bay leaf
15 g/½ oz flour
300 ml/½ pint chicken
  stock or liquid from
  canned tomatoes
salt and pepper
generous pinch sugar

1 Peel and dice the onion and carrot; skin and chop the tomatoes; remove the rind from the bacon and cut the rasher into small pieces.
2 Heat the butter and toss the diced onion, carrot and bacon in this; do not brown.
3 Add tomatoes and bay leaf and simmer (for a few minutes with canned tomatoes and rather longer with fresh tomatoes).

4 Blend the flour with the stock, add to the pan and simmer gently for about 30 minutes, stirring from time to time.
5 Rub through a sieve or liquidise, add seasoning and sugar and reheat.

Variations:
Devilled tomato sauce: Add 1–2 teaspoons curry powder, 1–2 teaspoons Worcestershire sauce and a few drops of Tabasco sauce at stage 4.

Spiced tomato sauce: Add ½ teaspoon mixed spice, ½ teaspoon ground cinnamon and ½ teaspoon ground nutmeg at stage 4.

Cranberry sauce

you will need for 4–6 servings:
METRIC/IMPERIAL
225–350 g/8–12 oz
  cranberries
150 ml/¼ pint water
50–75 g/2–3 oz sugar
25 g/1 oz butter

1 Simmer the cranberries in the water until softened.
2 Rub through a sieve or liquidise and add sugar to taste and butter.
3 For an unsieved sauce, make a syrup of the water and sugar, drop in the cranberries and cook until the mixture is thick.

Variations:
Glazed sauce: Add 2–3 tablespoons redcurrant or apple jelly at stage 1 or 3.

Orange and cranberry sauce: Add the finely grated rind and juice or pulp from 1–2 oranges to the cranberries at stage 1 or 3, or use orange jelly marmalade in place of sugar.

Port wine and cranberry sauce: Use port wine in place of all or some of the water.

Cumberland sauce

This sauce is excellent with chicken pâté or with cold chicken and ham.

you will need for 4–6 servings:
METRIC/IMPERIAL
1 orange
150 ml/¼ pint water
1 teaspoon arrowroot
6 tablespoons orange juice
2 tablespoons lemon juice
1–2 teaspoons made
  mustard
3 tablespoons port wine
6 tablespoons redcurrant
  jelly

1 Cut thin matchsticks of orange zest from the orange and soak in the water for 1 hour.
2 Simmer until tender and the water is reduced to 3 tablespoons.
3 Blend the arrowroot with the orange juice and lemon juice and add to the pan with the mustard, port wine and redcurrant jelly.
4 Stir over a low heat until clear and thickened. Serve hot or cold.

Stuffings

Stuffing chicken serves several purposes, among which is to provide additional flavour. Because chicken has a delicate flavour, it should not be stuffed with too strong a mixture. Stuffing also helps make the bird go further and helps keep the flesh moist.
For a small chicken, use one kind of stuffing for both neck and body. For a larger bird you can use one stuffing at the neck end and another stuffing in the body.
If the stuffing is put into the bird it will be cooked for the same time as the chicken. If you are cooking the stuffing separately, put it into an ovenproof dish, cover and cook. Judge the cooking time according to the softness of the ingredients used.

Freezing stuffings
It is better to freeze stuffings in a separate dish from the chicken, for this allows the chicken to be stored for a longer period. Most stuffings can be kept for a period of up to 3 months. Always wrap well so the mixture does not dry out. (For stuffings containing rice see page 56.)

Apple and raisin stuffing

you will need for 4–6 servings:

METRIC/IMPERIAL

I large cooking apple	50 g/2 oz soft
100 g/4 oz seedless	breadcrumbs
raisins	I small egg
I tablespoon chutney	salt and pepper

1 Peel, core and finely dice the apple.
2 Mix with the raisins, chutney, breadcrumbs, egg and seasoning.

Variation:
Apricot and raisin stuffing: Substitute 100 g/4 oz well drained chopped canned or cooked apricots for the apple. Omit the chutney and add 1 tablespoon chopped parsley.

Celery stuffing

you will need for 4–6 servings:

METRIC/IMPERIAL

I small head celery	2 tablespoons chopped
50 g/2 oz butter or	parsley
margarine	50 g/2 oz soft
salt and pepper	breadcrumbs or cooked
150 ml/¼ pint chicken	rice
stock	

1 Chop the celery neatly, discarding any tough outer sticks; chop a few leaves for extra flavour.
2 Heat the butter or margarine and toss the celery in it; add seasoning and stock.
3 Simmer for 10 minutes in an open pan until the celery has softened and the liquid has almost evaporated. Blend in the rest of the ingredients.

Variation:
Add chopped red and green pepper and 1–2 peeled and chopped onions with the celery at stage 2.

Chestnut stuffing

you will need for 4–6 servings:

METRIC/IMPERIAL

450 g/I lb chestnuts	25–50 g/I–2 oz butter or
50 g/2 oz soft	margarine
breadcrumbs	2 tablespoons milk or
salt and pepper	chicken stock

1 Split the chestnuts and boil in water to cover for about 10 minutes.
2 Remove the skins and simmer the nuts again in fresh water until very tender. Rub through a sieve or liquidise.
3 Add to the breadcrumbs, together with seasoning, butter or margarine and milk or stock.

Note:
Canned unsweetened chestnut purée can be substituted and stages 1 and 2 omitted.

Variations:
Bacon and chestnut stuffing: Add bacon rinds to the water at stage 2 and 100–175 g/4–6 oz chopped uncooked bacon with the breadcrumbs at stage 3.

Chestnut and hazelnut stuffing: Add 100 g/4 oz coarsely chopped hazelnuts, walnuts or peanuts at stage 3.

Chestnut and sausagemeat stuffing: Substitute 225–350 g/8–12 oz sausagemeat for the breadcrumbs at stage 3.

Ham and chestnut stuffing: Simmer the peeled chestnuts in ham stock at stage 2 and add 100 g/4 oz chopped ham to the chestnut purée at stage 3.

Forcemeat stuffing

you will need for 4–6 servings:

METRIC/IMPERIAL

225 g/8 oz sausagemeat	I tablespoon chopped
I egg	parsley
I teaspoon chopped fresh	
or ½ teaspoon dried	
mixed herbs	

1 Mix all ingredients together thoroughly.

Variations:
Celery forcemeat: Add 50–100 g/2–4 oz chopped raw celery.

Fruity forcemeat: Add 50 g/2 oz chopped nuts and

50–100 g/2–4 oz seedless raisins to the other ingredients.

Giblet forcemeat: Add the finely chopped cooked giblets of the chicken.

Vegetable forcemeat: Add 1 peeled grated onion, 1 diced red pepper (discarding core and seeds) and 1 peeled grated carrot.

Cream and liver stuffing

you will need for 4–8 servings:

METRIC/IMPERIAL

100 g/4 oz chicken livers	I tablespoon chopped parsley
50 g/2 oz butter	
50–100 g/2–4 oz mushrooms	100 g/4 oz soft breadcrumbs
150 ml/¼ pint double cream	salt and pepper
	I egg

1 Chop the chicken livers, melt the butter and slice the washed, unpeeled mushrooms.
2 Blend all the ingredients together.

Ham stuffing

you will need for 4–6 servings:

METRIC/IMPERIAL

25 g/I oz butter or margarine	I teaspoon chopped fresh or ½ teaspoon dried sage
225 g/8 oz cooked ham or boiled bacon	I teaspoon chopped fresh or ½ teaspoon dried thyme
75 g/3 oz soft breadcrumbs	150 ml/¼ pint chicken stock
I egg	
I tablespoon chopped parsley	

1 Heat the butter, chop the ham or bacon and blend both with the breadcrumbs.
2 Add the rest of the ingredients and mix well.

Variations:
Ham and cider stuffing: Substitute cider for chicken stock.

Ham and onion stuffing: Add 1 chopped onion fried in the hot butter before blending with the other ingredients.

Ham and rice stuffing

you will need for 4 servings:

METRIC/IMPERIAL

100 g/4 oz Patna type rice	50–75 g/2–3 oz ham or bacon
100 g/4 oz celery or I medium onion	I teaspoon chopped parsley
25 g/I oz butter	salt and pepper
½ teaspoon mixed herbs	I egg
cooked chicken liver	

1 Boil the rice in salted water until just tender.
2 Chop the celery or peeled onion finely; melt the butter and fry until softened.
3 Add to the well drained rice, together with the herbs, chopped liver, chopped ham and other ingredients. Mix well.

Sage and onion stuffing

you will need for 4–6 servings:

METRIC/IMPERIAL

2–3 large onions	I teaspoon dried or 2 teaspoons chopped fresh sage
300 ml/½ pint water	
salt and pepper	
75–100 g/3–4 oz breadcrumbs	I egg (optional)

1 Peel the onions and simmer in the water with seasoning until nearly soft.
2 Drain, reserving the stock, then chop and mix with the rest of the ingredients.
3 Bind with the onion stock or egg.

Mushroom stuffing

you will need for 4 servings:

METRIC/IMPERIAL

50 g/2 oz butter or margarine	100 g/4 oz soft breadcrumbs
I small onion	2 teaspoons chopped parsley
100 g/4 oz mushrooms	salt and pepper

1 Heat the butter or margarine and fry the finely chopped onion.
2 Add the finely chopped mushrooms (stalks as well), breadcrumbs, parsley and seasoning. Mix together thoroughly.

Parsley and thyme stuffing

This stuffing is particularly suitable for veal but could also be used for chicken.

you will need for 4 servings:

METRIC/IMPERIAL

50 g/2 oz shredded suet or melted butter or margarine	100 g/4 oz soft breadcrumbs
½ teaspoon mixed herbs	2–3 teaspoons chopped parsley
grated rind and juice of ½ lemon	salt and pepper

1 Mix all the ingredients thoroughly together.

Variations:
Giblet stuffing: Substitute cooked chopped giblets for the parsley.

Veal stuffing with bacon: Add 2–3 finely chopped bacon rashers.

Pineapple stuffing

you will need for 4–6 servings:

METRIC/IMPERIAL

4 large canned pineapple rings	3 tablespoons canned pineapple syrup
1 lemon	1 tablespoon chopped parsley
40 g/1½ oz butter	salt and pepper
50 g/2 oz soft breadcrumbs (preferably from brown bread)	

1 Chop the pineapple; grate the rind and squeeze out the juice from the lemon; melt the butter.
2 Mix all the ingredients together.

Variation:

Nutty pineapple stuffing: Add 50 g/2 oz chopped walnuts and 50–75 g/2–3 oz seedless raisins to the other ingredients.

Easy relishes

A relish is always served as an accompaniment to the bird, rather than as a stuffing inside. These dishes are equally good to serve with hot or cold chicken.

Beetroot relish

Mix together 225 g/8 oz diced cooked beetroot, 225 g/8 oz chopped celery heart, 50–75 g/2–3 oz chopped spring onions, 1 chopped green pepper (discarding core and seeds) and about 100 g/4 oz shredded cabbage heart. Moisten with French dressing (see page 80).

Cherry relish

Stone 450 g/1 lb Morello or other cherries. Put in a pan with 100 g/4 oz seedless raisins, 150 ml/¼ pint white malt vinegar, a generous pinch of ground cinnamon and sugar or honey to taste. Simmer until it becomes a thick mixture. Serve hot or cold with roasted chicken or turkey as well as duck.

Sweet corn relish

Peel and chop 1 large onion and toss in 25 g/1 oz melted butter until just soft, then blend with 225 g/8 oz cooked or well drained canned sweet corn, 1 chopped green and 1 chopped red pepper (discarding cores and seeds) and about 100 g/4 oz chopped cabbage heart. Moisten with French dressing (see page 80).

Cranberry rice relish

you will need for 4–8 servings:

METRIC/IMPERIAL

350 g/12 oz cooked rice	225 g/8 oz canned pineapple
225 ml/7½ fl oz Sauternes	225 g/8 oz sugar
450 g/1 lb fresh cranberries	225 g/8 oz mincemeat
2 oranges	225 g/8 oz walnuts or pecans

1 Leave rice to soak in the wine for about 3 hours.
2 Chop or mince the cranberries with the orange pulp.
3 Add the chopped pineapple, sugar, mincemeat and chopped nuts.
4 Leave to stand and chill while the rice marinates.
5 Combine the cranberry mixture with the marinated rice and serve cold.

Variation:

Apple cranberry relish: Substitute apple juice for Sauternes and diced cooked apples for the pineapple.

Stews and casseroles

There is probably more variety in stews and casserole dishes using chicken or fowl than almost any other type of food. It is because chicken blends so well with many different flavours; you can therefore produce different types of dishes for many varied occasions.

In many cases a particular type of chicken has been specified when this type gives the best result. If, however, you wish to substitute a boiling fowl for a young chicken in a casserole dish, you must allow approximately double the cooking time. You will need to add a little extra liquid because during the longer cooking period this will be absorbed.

Where vegetables are added, it may be advisable to cut them into rather larger pieces so they do not look overcooked and soft. On the other hand, if you substitute a young chicken for a boiling fowl, allow approximately half the recommended cooking time; you may need a little less liquid and to cut the vegetables into smaller pieces.

If using joints of frying chicken, instead of a boiling fowl, these of course are even more tender than a young roasting bird, so allow slightly under half the time given in the recipe. Vegetables should be cut into very small pieces. Wash and dry all chicken, removing any surplus fat from boiling fowls.

The giblets can be added to the chicken in some stews or casseroles but only where a very definite flavour already exists.

Adapting the cooking process

If you prefer to cook a stew in the oven instead of in a saucepan, all you need to do is *decrease* the amount of liquid by 25% as there is less loss due to evaporation. Cook in a cool to moderate oven (150–160°C, 300–325°F, Gas Mark 2–3) in a covered casserole, allowing about 20 minutes extra cooking time.

If, on the other hand, you want to cook the ingredients given for an oven casserole in a saucepan on top of the cooker, then *increase* the amount of liquid by 25%.

Freezing stews and casseroles

Most stews and casseroles freeze well after cooking. Since the food will need to be thoroughly reheated, do not overcook the first time. It is wise to leave thickening the mixture until reheating after freezing if possible.

Using a pressure cooker

Using a pressure cooker can save a great deal of time. If the recipe states that the food is browned first, do this in the open pan. Use about one-third less liquid than when cooking in a pan or casserole (you will not need the trivet).

Bring up to High (15 lb) pressure on a high heat, then lower the heat and allow about 5–7 minutes for dishes based on jointed young chicken, but 10–12 minutes for jointed older birds. Cool the pan under cold water.

Thickening should be done at the end of the cooking time, using the cooker as an open pan.

Chicken and tomato stew

serves 4

Halve 2 small young chickens or cut each into 4 portions. Skin 450 g/1 lb fresh tomatoes, peel and chop 2 medium onions and dice a canned or fresh red pepper (discarding the core and seeds of the latter). Heat 50 g/2 oz butter and fry the chicken for 5–10 minutes. Add the onion and pepper and cook for a further 10 minutes, then put in the tomatoes and 300 ml/½ pint chicken stock or water, 1–2 tablespoons tomato purée and seasoning. Simmer gently for 15–20 minutes and serve, garnished with chopped parsley.

Family casserole

you will need for 4 servings:

METRIC/IMPERIAL	
8 medium potatoes	salt and pepper
4 carrots	sprig of fresh or pinch
chopped celery	dried thyme
50 g/2 oz mushrooms	I bay leaf (optional)
4 onions	25 g/I oz butter
I chicken or fowl	(optional)
600 ml/I pint chicken	
stock	

1 Prepare and cut the vegetables into neat pieces or leave whole if cooking a boiling fowl.
2 Put the vegetables, chicken, giblets and stock into a casserole. (If using boiling fowl and thus cooking for a longer period, the potatoes should be added later). Add seasoning and herbs.
3 Spread the butter over the breast of a young lean chicken and cover the casserole.
4 Cook a younger chicken in the centre of a moderate oven (160°C, 325°F, Gas Mark 3), allowing 1½–1¾ hours; cook an older fowl for 2½–3 hours in a cool oven (150°C, 300°F, Gas Mark 2).
5 Lift the chicken and vegetables on to a serving dish and keep hot while preparing either a Velouté or Brown sauce (see pages 41 and 42) using the chicken stock.

Chicken bonne femme

you will need for 4–6 servings:

METRIC/IMPERIAL

1 boiling fowl	8 medium potatoes
100–175 g/4–6 oz fat bacon	salt and pepper
8 small onions or shallots	300 ml/½ pint chicken stock

1 The chicken may be either cut into joints or cooked whole. Cut the bacon into small pieces and peel the onions or shallots and potatoes, but leave them whole.
2 Fry the bacon until golden and put into a casserole; fry the onions or shallots in the bacon fat until golden brown.
3 Put the onions with the bacon in the casserole, then brown the chicken in the fat remaining in the pan. If necessary, add a little extra fat or butter, but do not make the chicken too greasy.
4 Put the chicken in the casserole on the bed of onions and bacon, seasoning lightly; do not add liquid.
5 Cover with a tightly fitting lid and cook for 1¼ hours for jointed boiling fowl or 2¼ hours for the whole bird in the centre of a cool to moderate oven (150–160°C, 300–325°F, Gas Mark 2–3); use the lower heat for the whole bird.
6 Spoon off any surplus fat, then add the potatoes, boiling stock and a little extra seasoning and continue cooking for a further 30 minutes.

Chicken casserole Provençale

you will need for 4–6 servings:

METRIC/IMPERIAL

1 small boiling fowl	25 g/1 oz flour
2–3 medium onions	50 g/2 oz chicken or cooking fat
4 carrots	
1–2 cloves garlic	300 ml/½ pint chicken stock
2–3 tomatoes	
salt and pepper	300 ml/½ pint red wine

to garnish:
black olives

1 Cut the boiling fowl into neat joints.
2 Peel and dice the onions and carrots; crush the garlic; skin and slice the tomatoes.
3 Coat the chicken joints with seasoned flour and brown in the hot fat in a pan. Remove the chicken to a casserole.
4 Put the onions, garlic and tomatoes into the fat remaining in the pan and cook for a few minutes until the vegetables are lightly browned.
5 Add the stock and wine and bring to the boil, stirring until slightly thickened, then add the carrots and simmer for 5 minutes.
6 Pour over the chicken in the casserole, cover tightly and cook in a cool oven (150°C, 300°F, Gas Mark 2) for 2½–3 hours. Just before serving add the olives.

Variations:

Casserole Dijon: Omit the red wine and use 600 ml/ 1 pint chicken stock at stage 5. Blend about 1 tablespoon (to taste) of Dijon mustard into the stock together with 2 tablespoons chopped parsley and 2 teaspoons capers.

Cinnamon chicken: Substitute white wine for the red wine and tomatoes. Blend 1 teaspoon ground cinnamon with the flour at stage 3. When the casserole is cooked, omit black olives and top with yogurt. Sprinkle ground cinnamon and chopped parsley over the top before serving.

Chicken Chasseur sauce

Although this is an excellent sauce in which to reheat cooked chicken you can also use it for cooking raw chicken.

you will need for 4 servings:

METRIC/IMPERIAL
for the sauce:

1 large tomato	25 g/1 oz flour
1 onion	600 ml/1 pint chicken or brown stock
1 carrot	
2–3 mushrooms	salt and pepper
50 g/2 oz chicken fat or dripping	

1 Skin and chop the tomato, onion and carrot; wipe or wash the mushrooms and slice neatly.
2 Heat the fat and toss the vegetables in it for several minutes. Add the flour and stir over a low heat for 2–3 minutes.
3 Blend in the stock, season well then simmer in a covered pan for about 45 minutes until the sauce has thickened and the vegetables are very tender. This sauce should not be sieved or liquidised.

To use with cooked chicken: Add the portions of cooked chicken to the thickened sauce and simmer gently or heat in a covered casserole until the chicken is thoroughly reheated.

To use with young chicken joints: Brown the chicken joints first at stage 2 in a little hot fat then lift out of the pan and add any extra fat required. Simmer the sauce for about 15 minutes only at stage 3, until the vegetables begin to soften. Add the chicken joints and continue cooking in a tightly covered pan for another 30 minutes.

To use with boiling chicken joints: Remove surplus fat from the bird and joint. Fry as above for young chicken joints and remove from the pan. Use 900 ml/ 1½ pints stock at stage 3. When the sauce has thickened, add the chicken joints then simmer very gently in a tightly covered pan for about 1¼ hours.

Chicken goulash (1)

you will need for 6–8 servings:

METRIC/IMPERIAL
I medium boiling fowl	bouquet garni
2 large onions	salt and pepper
I clove garlic	I tablespoon paprika
50 g/2 oz lard or chicken fat	300 ml/½ pint chicken stock (with canned tomatoes) or 450 ml/¾ pint stock (with fresh tomatoes)
I (397-g/14-oz) can tomatoes or 450 g/I lb tomatoes	

1 Cut the fowl into neat portions; discard the surplus fat often found on boiling fowls.
2 Peel and slice the onions and crush the garlic.
3 Melt the lard or chicken fat and cook the onions and garlic in it for a few minutes.
4 Add the chicken joints, tomatoes, bouquet garni, salt, pepper and paprika and cook for 5 minutes.
5 Transfer to a casserole, add the stock and cook in the centre of a cool oven (140°C, 275°F, Gas Mark 1) for 3 hours. Remove bouquet garni and serve with boiled noodles or rice.

Variation:

Chicken goulash (2): Add 4–6 medium peeled, thickly sliced potatoes to the chicken mixture at stage 4. The amount of paprika could be increased to 1½–2 tablespoons.

Chicken stew

you will need for 4–6 servings:

METRIC/IMPERIAL
I chicken or fowl	salt and pepper
75 g/3 oz fat bacon	25 g/I oz flour
I large onion	300 ml/½ pint milk
175–225 g/6–8 oz mixed root vegetables	25 g/I oz butter (optional)
600 ml/I pint chicken stock or water	

to garnish:
chopped parsley

1 Cut the chicken into 8 neat pieces (2 joints from each leg and 2 from breast and wings).
2 Dice the bacon; peel and dice the vegetables.
3 Put the chicken and vegetables into a large pan and add the stock or water and seasoning.
4 Put on the lid and simmer gently for about 2 hours until the chicken is tender. If using a young chicken, allow 1 hour only.
5 Blend the flour with the milk and stir into the liquid; add the butter if used. Bring to the boil, stirring well, and cook until smooth and thickened.
6 Taste and add more seasoning if necessary, and garnish with chopped parsley.

Variations:

Chicken in mustard sauce: Add ½–1 tablespoon dry mustard to the flour at stage 5 and 3 tablespoons double cream at stage 6.

Chicken with nuts: Omit the root vegetables and add 100 g/4 oz skinned chopped nuts (of any kind) at stage 5 and 2–3 tablespoons cream at stage 6.

Waterzoi: Add 1 crushed clove of garlic at stage 3 and 100 g/4 oz mushrooms towards the end of the stage 4 cooking period. Blend 2 egg yolks with 150 ml/¼ pint double cream and whisk into the hot, but not boiling, liquid at stage 6. Stir over a low heat until thickened. Top with chopped chives as well as parsley.

Hotpot of chicken

you will need for 4–6 servings:

METRIC/IMPERIAL
8 medium potatoes	about 150 ml/¼ pint chicken stock
4–5 medium onions	25 g/I oz butter or margarine
I chicken or fowl	
salt and pepper	

1 Peel and slice the potatoes and onions; if cooking a young bird these must be sliced very thinly, but could be thicker if cooking the older bird for a longer period.
2 Joint the chicken or fowl, cutting away any surplus fat from the latter; it is easier to eat the hotpot if you remove leg bones, but do not waste any of the pieces of chicken (scrape the bones well). The stock in the recipe can be made with the giblets.
3 Put a layer of sliced potatoes and onions into a casserole, cover with the chicken, then add the seasoned stock; use only enough to half-cover the layer of chicken or the hotpot will be too moist.
4 Put the rest of the onions over the chicken, season and add the final layer of potatoes.
5 Melt the butter or margarine and spread or spoon over the potatoes; season lightly.
6 Cover the casserole and cook in the centre of a moderate oven (160°C, 325°F, Gas Mark 3) for 1½–1¾ hours for a younger bird, but 2½–3 hours in a cool oven (150°C, 300°F, Gas Mark 2) for an older fowl. Remove the lid for the last 30 minutes of cooking time so the potatoes can brown and crisp.

Variations:

Hotpot Niçoise: Add 4 large skinned, sliced tomatoes, plus 1–2 crushed cloves of garlic to the layers of onions.

Irish hotpot: Substitute Guinness for the stock and add sliced carrots to the other vegetables.

Chicken and mushroom casserole

you will need for 6–8 servings:

METRIC/IMPERIAL
4 joints chicken	225 g/8 oz mushrooms
salt and pepper	50 g/2 oz butter or
25 g/1 oz flour	chicken fat
12 small shallots or	450 ml/¾ pint chicken
pickling onions	stock

1 Roll the chicken joints in well seasoned flour.
2 Peel the shallots or onions; wipe or wash but do not peel the mushrooms.
3 Heat the butter or fat in a pan. Fry the chicken until golden brown then transfer to a casserole with the shallots or onions and mushrooms.
4 Blend the stock into any butter and flour remaining in the pan. Bring to the boil and cook until thickened.
5 Pour over the chicken, cover the casserole and cook in a moderate oven (160°C, 325°F, Gas Mark 3) for approximately 1 hour.

Variation:
Add 1–2 tablespoons chopped tarragon at stage 3.

Creamy casseroled chicken

you will need for 4 servings:

METRIC/IMPERIAL
2 onions	300 ml/½ pint single
2 potatoes	cream or evaporated
1 carrot	milk
1 small boiling fowl	150 ml/¼ pint chicken
65 g/2½ oz butter or	stock
margarine	salt and pepper
25 g/1 oz flour	

+ 1 cup red wine

1 Peel and slice the vegetables and cut the chicken into joints.
2 Melt the butter or margarine, fry the vegetables lightly and remove from the pan.
3 Fry the chicken until lightly browned and remove.
4 Add the flour to the fat remaining in the pan and cook for a few minutes, stirring.
5 Add the cream or evaporated milk and the chicken stock. Bring to the boil and stir until thickened.
6 Season the sauce; put the chicken and vegetables into a casserole and pour the sauce over.
7 Cook in the centre of a moderate oven (160°C, 325°F, Gas Mark 3) for 2 hours. Remove lid and cook for a further 10 minutes until the sauce is lightly browned.

Very good.

Chicken and tomato casserole

you will need for 4 servings:

METRIC/IMPERIAL
4 joints chicken	50 g/2 oz butter or
salt and pepper	margarine or 2
2 onions	tablespoons oil
450 g/1 lb tomatoes	300 ml/½ pint chicken
	stock
	2 bay leaves

to garnish:
triangles of fried bread
   or crisp toast

1 Season the chicken joints well; peel and slice the onions and tomatoes.
2 Heat the butter, margarine or oil and fry the chicken joints for 5 minutes until golden brown. Lift out of the pan and put into a casserole.
3 Fry the onions in any fat or oil left in the pan; add the tomatoes, stock, bay leaves and seasoning. Simmer for 5 minutes or until the tomatoes begin to soften.
4 Pour over the chicken and put the lid on the casserole. Cook in the centre of a moderate oven (160°C, 325°F, Gas Mark 3) for 1 hour.
5 Remove the bay leaves and serve from the casserole, garnished with triangles of fried bread or crisp toast.

Note:
If using an older bird, steam or simmer for about 1–1¼ hours then joint and continue as stage 1.

Variation:
Slimmers' casserole: Omit stage 2. Simmer the vegetables with the stock, herbs and seasoning. Put into the casserole with the raw chicken joints as stage 4. Garnish with chopped parsley instead of croûtons.

Southern chicken casserole

you will need for 4 servings:

METRIC/IMPERIAL
1 small boiling fowl	1 large onion
4 medium potatoes	1 (397-g/14-oz) can
1 medium cooking apple	tomatoes
salt and pepper	2 teaspoons brown sugar
25 g/1 oz flour	1–2 teaspoons made
25–50 g/1–2 oz dripping	mustard
or cooking fat	

1 Joint the boiling fowl; peel the potatoes and slice; peel, core and slice the apple.
2 Coat the chicken with seasoned flour and brown in the melted dripping or fat (use the smaller amount if the bird is very fatty). Remove from the pan.
3 Peel and slice the onion and fry in the remaining fat; add the tomatoes plus the liquid from the can, sugar, mustard and seasoning and heat for 5 minutes.
4 Arrange the potato slices in the bottom of a greased

casserole, add the apple slices then the tomato mixture.

5 Top with the browned chicken joints, cover the casserole and bake in the centre of a moderate oven (160°C, 325°F, Gas Mark 3) for 2–2¼ hours or until tender.

Note:
This is very good served with cream slaw (see page 81) or pickled beetroot.

Spiced chicken casserole

you will need for 4–6 servings:

METRIC/IMPERIAL

I small boiling fowl	450 ml/¾ pint chicken stock
½ teaspoon curry powder	I tablespoon Worcestershire sauce
½ teaspoon paprika	
½ teaspoon mixed spice	I tablespoon vinegar
salt and pepper	8 small onions
25 g/1 oz flour	225 g/8 oz diced celery
50 g/2 oz fat	I clove garlic (optional)

1 Cut the fowl into neat joints. Mix seasonings with the flour and roll the chicken in it.
2 Fry in hot fat for a few minutes, then place in a casserole.
3 Add the stock, Worcestershire sauce and vinegar to the fat and flour left in the pan. Bring to the boil and cook for several minutes.
4 Peel the onions and put into the casserole with the diced celery; cover chicken and vegetables with the sauce, adding the crushed clove of garlic if desired.
5 Cover and cook for 2½ hours in a cool oven (150°C, 300°F, Gas Mark 2).

Variation:
Sweet-sour casserole: Omit the curry powder and mixed spice at stage 1.

Mexican-style chicken with peppers

you will need for 4 servings:

METRIC/IMPERIAL

I–1·25-kg/2–2½-lb chicken	I tablespoon vinegar
salt and pepper	150 ml/¼ pint medium sherry
50 g/2 oz fat	
I large clove garlic	3 cloves
I large onion	1–2 large green peppers
25 g/1 oz flour	I tablespoon raisins
200 ml/⅓ pint water	12 green olives
I tablespoon tomato purée	sugar to taste

1 Quarter the chicken and season; melt the fat in a frying pan, lightly brown the chicken joints on each side, then lift out and transfer to a casserole.
2 Peel and crush the garlic, slice the onion and fry gently in the remaining fat.

3 Stir in the flour; when it begins to brown, add the water and tomato purée, vinegar and sherry.
4 Stir over the heat until smooth. Add the cloves and sliced green peppers (discarding the core and seeds). Pour this sauce over the chicken.
5 Cover and cook in the centre of a moderate oven (180°C, 350°F, Gas Mark 4) for 40–45 minutes.
6 Add the raisins and the stoned, chopped olives, sugar and extra seasoning 20 minutes before the end of the cooking time. Serve with boiled rice.

Chicken and prunes

you will need for 6–8 servings:

METRIC/IMPERIAL

100–175 g/4–6 oz prunes	I large roasting chicken
450 ml/¾ pint chicken stock or water	I chicken liver
	2 bay leaves
2 large onions	I tablespoon vinegar
50 g/2 oz chicken or cooking fat	salt and pepper
	2 tablespoons redcurrant jelly
50 g/2 oz flour	
300 ml/½ pint red wine	

to garnish:
fried croûtons

1 Soak the prunes overnight in the stock or water. Drain and reserve the liquid.
2 Peel and chop the onions, then heat the fat in a very large pan and toss the onions in it; do not allow them to brown.
3 Stir in the flour and cook until golden brown. Gradually add the wine and reserved stock or water from the prunes; bring to the boil, stirring, and cook until smooth.
4 Add the whole chicken, chicken liver, bay leaves, vinegar and prunes.
5 Simmer gently for about 1½ hours; season to taste.
6 Remove the liver and rub it through a sieve, liquidise or chop. Return it to the sauce with the redcurrant jelly. Simmer for a further 15 minutes to melt the jelly.
7 Re-season if necessary or add a little more redcurrant jelly.
8 Remove bay leaves before serving and garnish with crisp croûtons of fried bread. Serve with redcurrant jelly.

Chicken tetrazzini

you will need for 6–8 servings:

METRIC/IMPERIAL

I small chicken or fowl	I medium onion
2 teaspoons salt	I large green pepper
¼ teaspoon pepper	I large red pepper
3 rashers bacon	225 g/8 oz spaghetti
50–100 g/2–4 oz mushrooms	100 g/4 oz hard cheese

1 Cut the chicken or fowl into pieces, put into a pan with water to cover and season well.
2 Simmer until the meat loosens from the bones (this will take 1–2 hours depending upon the bird).
3 Remove meat from the bones and cut into small dice. Reserve the stock.
4 Chop the bacon and mushrooms; peel and chop the onion.
5 Fry the bacon in a pan for 2–3 minutes until the fat runs, then add the mushrooms and onion and cook until nearly tender.
6 Dice the peppers, discarding cores and seeds, and add to the bacon mixture; continue cooking for 10 minutes.
7 Boil the spaghetti in the reserved chicken liquid for 15 minutes or until just tender, then lift from the pan with a perforated spoon (save the liquid again) and blend with the bacon mixture.
8 Add the diced chicken and enough reserved chicken stock to moisten and heat thoroughly.
9 Grate the cheese and blend into the mixture just before serving.

The following recipes are for curries; remember that the amount of curry powder and/or paste used is a matter of personal taste. Add sparingly until you are sure of the amount you like.

For accompaniments to curries, serve chutney, sliced fruit (bananas, oranges, apples), gherkins and small onions, rings of green pepper and tomato, yogurt blended with strips of cucumber, nuts, raisins, poppadums and/or Bombay duck.

Chicken curry (I)

you will need for 4 servings:
METRIC/IMPERIAL
450 g/1 lb cooked chicken
350 g/12 oz onions
1 clove garlic
1 small apple
50 g/2 oz chicken dripping or fat
½–1 tablespoon curry powder
½ tablespoon flour

300 ml/½ pint chicken stock
1 teaspoon tomato purée
½ tablespoon lemon juice
1 tablespoon condensed milk or sweet chutney
1 tablespoon desiccated coconut
2 tablespoons sultanas
salt and pepper

1 Cut the chicken into neat pieces (do not discard odd pieces of skin, or stuffing if using roast chicken).
2 Peel and chop the onions, garlic and apple.
3 Heat the dripping or fat and fry the onion and garlic for several minutes.
4 Add the chopped apple. Stir in the curry powder and flour, then the stock.
5 Add the rest of the ingredients, except the chicken; cover the pan and simmer for 20 minutes.
6 Add the chicken and heat thoroughly. Serve with boiled rice and accompaniments.

Variations:
Chicken curry (2): If using uncooked chicken omit stage 1. Use 600 ml/1 pint of chicken stock at stage 4. Simmer the diced or jointed uncooked chicken with the rest of the ingredients for 1–1¼ hours for young chicken or up to 2–2¼ hours for older boiling fowl. If you can make the curry one day and reheat it another it has a better flavour.

For a hotter flavour: Add 1–2 teaspoons curry paste at stage 4.

Fruity curry: Add 1 tablespoon chutney and 1 tablespoon plum or other sweet jam at stage 5. This is particularly good with Chicken curry (2).

Chicken Vindaloo: Omit stage 1. Omit the curry powder and apple and substitute 1 teaspoon turmeric, ¼–½ teaspoon chilli powder and a small piece of root ginger (chopped finely). Boil 6 medium potatoes until just firm or bake in their jackets and skin. Slice or halve and put into a dish. Prepare and fry the onions and garlic as stages 2 and 3, blend with the turmeric, chilli and ginger, spoon over the potatoes and leave for 1–2 hours. Meanwhile skin and fry 3–4 tomatoes and 1–2 extra cloves of finely chopped garlic. Add a jointed young chicken (remove as many bones as possible) and fry until golden, then add the stock and cook gently for 1 hour. Blend in the potato mixture and heat through.

Madras chicken

you will need for 4 servings:
METRIC/IMPERIAL
1 large aubergine
salt
½ teaspoon curry powder
50 g/2 oz mushrooms

1 clove garlic
1 onion
75 g/3 oz butter
4 frying chicken breasts

for the sauce:
25 g/1 oz butter
25 g/1 oz flour or 15 g/½ oz cornflour
1 teaspoon curry powder
150 ml/¼ pint chicken stock

150 ml/¼ pint white wine
4 tablespoons double cream
salt and pepper

1 Wipe the aubergine but do not peel; slice thinly. Sprinkle with salt (it draws out the juices and eliminates the bitter taste of the skin). Leave for 15–20 minutes, pat slices dry and sprinkle with the curry powder.
2 Slice the mushrooms, peel and chop the garlic and onion. Heat two-thirds of the butter and fry the vegetables until soft. Put in an ovenproof serving dish and keep hot.
3 Fry the chicken breasts in the remaining third of the butter until tender and arrange on the vegetables.
4 For the sauce, heat the butter and stir in the flour or cornflour and curry powder. Blend in the stock and bring the thickened sauce to the boil: whisk in the

wine and cream. Season and cook gently without boiling until smooth and thick. Spoon over the chicken breasts. Serve with rice and green salad.

Creamed chicken curry

serves 4

Make 300 ml/½ pint creamed curry sauce (see page 43) and lower heat or transfer to the top of a double saucepan. Cut 350–450 g/12 oz–1 lb cooked chicken into neat pieces and add to the sauce with 2 tablespoons cream; heat gently. Garnish with chopped parsley and hard-boiled egg. Serve with boiled rice and chutney.

Sate Ajam

serves 4

This is a delicious adaptation of the Indonesian dish, usually cooked on skewers. Peel and crush 2 cloves of garlic and chop 2 onions, blend with ½–1 teaspoon chilli powder, 1–2 tablespoons soya sauce and pour over a jointed young chicken. Leave for 1 hour. Fry another chopped onion in 2 tablespoons oil and add 300 ml/½ pint coconut milk or 1 tablespoon desiccated coconut and 300 ml/½ pint chicken stock, 1 tablespoon lemon juice and the chicken mixture. Simmer gently until tender (about 40 minutes), then add 50–75 g/2–3 oz peanuts, 1 tablespoon peanut butter and seasoning to taste.

Coq au vin

Although this is a casserole of chicken, it is *not* a way of cooking an elderly boiling fowl. A young, plump cock should be used. The dish could be made with 300 ml/½ pint chicken stock and 300 ml/½ pint wine if a less strong taste is desired. Some cooks prefer a white rather than a red wine.

you will need for 4–6 servings:

METRIC/IMPERIAL
100 g/4 oz mushrooms	50–75 g/2–3 oz butter or oil
8 small shallots or onions	
1 or more cloves garlic	25 g/1 oz flour
100 g/4 oz fat bacon or pork	600 ml/1 pint red wine
	salt and pepper
1 young chicken (cock bird)	

1 Slice the mushrooms; peel the shallots or onions and leave whole. Peel and crush the garlic (to taste). Dice the bacon or pork and joint the chicken.
2 Fry the vegetables, garlic and bacon in the butter or oil until golden brown; remove from the pan, add the chicken and cook until golden, then lift out of the pan.
3 Stir the flour into the butter remaining in the pan, cook for 3–4 minutes, then gradually add the wine, bringing just to the boil and simmering until smooth.
4 Return the chicken and vegetable mixture to the sauce, season well and simmer for approximately 30 minutes until the chicken is tender.

Variations:
Devonshire chicken: Omit the mushrooms, shallots or small onions, garlic and fat bacon or pork. Substitute 4–6 sharp dessert apples and 1 large onion and carrot. Cook the chicken in 50 g/2 oz butter only at stage 2. Add the peeled sliced onion, carrot and 2 peeled sliced apples; fry in the butter left in the pan and season well. Add 15 g/½ oz flour and 300 ml/½ pint cider. Bring to the boil, add the chicken joints and simmer for 25–30 minutes. Meanwhile peel and quarter the remaining apples, brown lightly in 25 g/1 oz butter and add 4 tablespoons water; simmer until just soft. Lift the chicken on to a dish, add 150 ml/¼ pint double cream to the sauce, heat gently then spoon or strain over the chicken. Add softened apple quarters and chopped parsley.

Hasty coq au vin: Joint a cooked chicken. Drain 12–18 cocktail onions. Dice 2–3 rashers of bacon and wipe 100 g/4 oz small mushrooms. Heat 50 g/2 oz butter and fry the onions and bacon until golden; blend in 15 g/½ oz flour. Stir in 450 ml/¾ pint red or white wine. Bring to the boil, add the chicken and mushrooms and simmer in the pan for 20 minutes.

Chicken in spiced vinegar

This is based on Hasenpfeffer, a dish generally made with rabbit or hare, but it is equally good with chicken.

you will need for 4–6 servings:

METRIC/IMPERIAL
1 roasting chicken	50 g/2 oz fat
600 ml/1 pint vinegar	6 cloves
1 onion	½ tablespoon mustard seeds
salt and pepper	
600 ml/1 pint water	3 bay leaves
40 g/1½ oz flour	sugar

1 Cut the chicken into joints; soak overnight in the vinegar, onion, seasoning and water.
2 Strain, dry and coat the chicken joints in half the flour.
3 Fry the chicken in the hot fat until golden brown then add the vinegar liquid, the spices, bay leaves and a little sugar; simmer for approximately 1 hour.
4 Blend the rest of the flour with a little water, add to the liquid and cook until thickened.
5 Arrange the joints on a hot dish and pour over the strained sauce. Serve with dumplings, cooked in salted water in a separate pan (see page 19).

Djaja mammra

The semolina used in this dish is very coarse (ask for semolina for couscous), almost like a small rice grain. Ras el Hanout is a traditional Moorish spice which is composed of a number of ingredients, including mixed spice, cinnamon, pimento, black pepper, ginger etc. It is very hot. If not available, blend a little curry powder, ginger, black pepper, cinnamon and mixed spice together.

you will need for 6–8 servings:

METRIC/IMPERIAL

75 g/3 oz coarse semolina	pinch salt
50 g/2 oz blanched almonds	I large roasting chicken or tender boiling fowl
75 g/3 oz butter	pinch ground ginger
100 g/4 oz raisins	1–2 onions
½–I teaspoon Ras el Hanout (or to taste)	pinch saffron powder

1 First cook the semolina: tie in muslin, allowing room for it to swell in cooking, put in a steamer over a pan of boiling water and cook for about 25 minutes until tender.
2 Chop the almonds and mix with the semolina, one-third of the butter, raisins, Ras el Hanout and salt to taste; put this stuffing into the chicken and tie or skewer firmly.
3 Place the chicken in a heavy saucepan with water to half cover. Add the rest of the ingredients, including the remaining butter.
4 Boil steadily in a covered pan for about 1 hour then remove the lid and finish cooking in an open pan so that the water evaporates (see note below), leaving only butter and chicken fat in the base of the pan. Then turn the chicken in the butter over a steady heat until brown.
5 Serve the chicken with the stuffing and any buttery sauce left in the pan.

Note:

The above is the traditional Moroccan method, but I leave a little liquid in the pan at stage 4, pour this off into another pan and thicken it for a sauce.

Rice and Pasta Dishes

Rice

A number of recipes in this book use cooked rice, since it is a very good accompaniment to any type of chicken dish. There are several ways in which it can be cooked, and these are given on the following pages. Patna or long-grain rice is used for savoury dishes.

In order to prepare the right amount without any wastage, you can assume that rice approximately doubles or even trebles its weight in cooking. So if a recipe calls for 100 g/4 oz cooked rice, you need 40–50 g/1½–2 oz raw rice.

It used to be considered that all rice should be washed before being cooked. Today, with the careful selection and pre-packing of rice, it is thought advisable *not* to wash any but brown rice because some of the food value would be lost. If, however, you buy rice loose or in sacks, washing in cold water is advisable, but cook as quickly as possible after washing to prevent rice becoming sticky.

Freezing rice dishes

Cool the mixture then freeze *lightly*. Separate rice, etc. with a fork or your hand if frozen in a polythene bag. This prevents the rice mixture forming a solid block. Reheat from frozen in hot chicken stock or defrost and heat in a little butter. Use plain cooked rice within 4–5 months, but most rice dishes containing chicken, etc. should be used within 2 months.

Boiled rice (1)

you will need for 4 servings:

METRIC/IMPERIAL
1 litre 150 ml/2 pints water
1 teaspoon salt

100 g/4 oz Patna or long-grain rice

1 Bring the water to the boil and add salt, then the rice.
2 Cook steadily until tender, approximately 15 minutes. The grains of rice should be soft but unbroken.
3 If time permits, rinse through a sieve with cold water and reheat on a flat tray or in the sieve over boiling water; if short of time, rinse in boiling water. This gets rid of excess starch.

Boiled rice (2)

Use a smaller amount of water for quick-cooking or tenderised rice. You need 2–2½ times the amount of water to rice. If you use a teacup for measuring the rice, it is important that you use the same cup for measuring the water.

you will need for 4 servings:

METRIC/IMPERIAL
2–2½ teacups or 300–375 ml/½–⅔ pint water

1 teaspoon salt
1 teacup or 150 g/5 oz Patna or long-grain rice

1 Put the cold water, salt and rice together in the pan.
2 Bring to the boil and stir briskly.
3 Put lid on the pan and turn heat to low.
4 Leave for 15 minutes, by which time the rice will have absorbed all the water and every grain should be separate.

Steamed rice

you will need for 4 servings:

METRIC/IMPERIAL
1 teacup or 150 g/5 oz Patna or long-grain rice
2 teacups or 300 ml/½ pint water

salt to taste

1 Put the rice, water and salt in the top of a double saucepan or basin over boiling water. Cover with foil or a lid.
2 Cook until all the water has been absorbed, about 25 minutes.

Flavourings for rice

Use the following with any method of cooking rice:

Saffron: Either infuse about 12 strands of saffron in the water or other liquid for 1 hour before cooking the rice, strain if desired and continue as recipe, or blend from a pinch to 1 teaspoon powdered saffron with the liquid before cooking.

Savoury: Use stock in place of water.

Rice Lyonnaise: Add a finely chopped onion to the liquid or fry the onion in hot oil or fat then add to the rice and continue as the recipe.

Tomato rice: Add 2 skinned chopped tomatoes to the rice before cooking, or cook in tomato juice, or tomato juice plus water or stock instead of all water.

Vegetable risotto: Fry a chopped onion, 50 g/2 oz sliced mushrooms and 1–2 skinned chopped tomatoes in hot oil or fat then add to the rice and proceed as the recipe.

Fried rice: Cook the rice, taking care not to overcook. Allow to dry on absorbent paper then fry in hot oil or fat until golden in colour.

Curry-flavoured rice: Either add from a pinch to 1 tablespoon curry powder to the liquid or fry a chopped onion and then 1–4 teaspoons curry powder in a little hot oil or fat, add to the rice and proceed as the recipe.

Chicken pilaff (1)

you will need for 4 servings:

METRIC/IMPERIAL

1 onion	salt and pepper
2 large tomatoes	1 teaspoon sugar
25 g/1 oz almonds	600 ml/1 pint chicken
225 g/8 oz medium **or**	stock
long-grain rice	225–350 g/8–12 oz
50 g/2 oz butter	cooked chicken
50 g/2 oz currants	

1 Peel and chop the onion and tomatoes; blanch and chop the almonds.
2 Fry the rice in melted butter for 2–3 minutes, add the onion, tomatoes, nuts, currants, seasoning and sugar; pour in the stock and stir well.
3 Cover tightly with a lid and cook on a low heat for about 20 minutes or until the stock is completely absorbed; stir several times while cooking.
4 Dice the chicken and add to the rice mixture when nearly cooked; heat through.

Variation:

Chicken pilaff (2): Omit the nuts and add 50–75 g/ 2–3 oz sultanas and 1 chopped green pepper (discarding core and seeds) at stage 2.

Chicken kedgeree

you will need for 4 servings:

METRIC/IMPERIAL

1 onion	450 ml/¾ pint chicken
350 g/12 oz cooked	stock or water
chicken	salt and pepper
50 g/2 oz butter	2 eggs
175 g/6 oz Patna or	chopped parsley
long-grain rice	

1 Peel and slice or chop the onion and dice the chicken.
2 Heat the butter in a pan and fry the onion for several minutes, then add the rice and turn in the onion mixture until well coated.
3 Add the stock or water and seasoning to taste; bring to the boil, lower the heat, cover the pan and simmer for 10 minutes.
4 Meanwhile hard-boil the eggs.
5 Add the chicken and a little chopped parsley to the rice and continue cooking for a further 5–6 minutes.
6 Shell the eggs, chop the whites and stir into the chicken mixture.
7 Pile on to a hot serving dish and garnish with sieved or chopped egg yolks and a little more parsley.

Variation:

Cream chicken kedgeree: Add 4–6 tablespoons

double cream to the rice and chicken with the egg whites at stage 6. The onion may be omitted; use a slightly smaller amount of stock.

Risotto with chicken

you will need for 4 servings:

METRIC/IMPERIAL

1 onion	salt and pepper
65 g/2½ oz butter	225 g/8 oz cooked
225 g/8 oz Italian or	chicken
long-grain rice	50–75 g/2–3 oz hard
1 litre 150 ml/2 pints	cheese
chicken stock	

1 Peel and chop the onion finely and fry in about half the butter until soft and transparent; add the rice and stir for 1–2 minutes until coated.
2 Pour in the stock, add seasoning and stir; bring to the boil.
3 Cover and cook over a low heat for about 20 minutes until the rice is tender and all the liquid absorbed.
4 Chop the chicken and grate the cheese, then add to the rice mixture with the rest of the butter; heat through gently.

Variations:

Chicken and vegetable risotto: Add 50–75 g/2–3 oz sliced mushrooms to the onion at stage 1. Add 100–175 g/4–6 oz cooked peas at stage 4.

Curried risotto: Blend 1 tablespoon curry powder with the onion at stage 1. Add 50 g/2 oz sultanas at stage 4 and omit the cheese.

Pasta

Pasta should never be overcooked and it is important to use sufficient liquid. Allow 1 litre 150 ml/2 pints liquid to each 100 g/4 oz pasta. Bring the water or other liquid to the boil, season to taste, then add the pasta and cook fairly quickly. Drain the pasta as soon as it is cooked, except for dishes where this is not practicable.

Never overcook pasta when it is to be frozen as this spoils the texture. If preparing chicken with lasagne *especially* for freezing, follow any special directions at the end of the recipe. Use most pasta dishes within 2 months.

Fried noodles

you will need for 4 servings:

METRIC/IMPERIAL

1 litre 150 ml/2 pints	salt
water	100 g/4 oz noodles

to fry:
oil or fat

1 Bring water to the boil and add up to 1 teaspoon salt.
2 Add the noodles and cook for 10 minutes until almost tender, taking care not to overcook; separate carefully during cooking with a spoon, then drain and dry on absorbent paper or cloth.
3 Heat a 5-mm/¼-inch layer of oil or fat in a strong frying pan or a pan of deep oil or fat plus the frying basket. Fry the noodles until crisp and brown. If using shallow oil or fat, cook only a few noodles at a time and keep hot in the oven.
4 Drain on absorbent paper.

Spaghetti with chicken sauce

you will need for 4 servings:

METRIC/IMPERIAL

2 medium onions	salt and pepper
1–2 cloves garlic	350 g/12 oz spaghetti
2–3 tomatoes	50–75 g/2–3 oz Parmesan
450 g/1 lb cooked chicken	cheese
50 g/2 oz butter	50 g/2 oz melted butter
300 ml/½ pint water	
2 tablespoons tomato purée	

1 Peel and chop the onions, crush the garlic, and skin and slice the tomatoes; cut the chicken into neat pieces.
2 Heat the butter and cook the onions and garlic until golden brown.
3 Add the chicken, cook gently for 5 minutes then stir in the water, tomatoes, tomato purée and seasoning.
4 Cover the pan and simmer for 20 minutes, stirring once or twice.
5 Meanwhile cook the spaghetti in boiling salted water for about 15 minutes; grate the cheese.
6 When the spaghetti is cooked, drain, toss in melted butter and serve with the chicken sauce poured over. Serve with the cheese in a separate dish.

Chicken and macaroni cheese

you will need for 4–6 servings:

METRIC/IMPERIAL

75 g/3 oz macaroni	225 g/8 oz cooked
salt	chicken

for the sauce:

100 g/4 oz Cheddar cheese	450 ml/¾ pint milk or mixed chicken stock and milk
40 g/1½ oz butter or margarine	salt and pepper
40 g/1½ oz flour	

for the topping:

50 g/2 oz Cheddar cheese	15–25 g/½–1 oz butter or margarine
25–50 g/1–2 oz soft breadcrumbs	

1 Cook the macaroni in boiling well salted water until just tender, then drain.
2 Meanwhile, dice the chicken and grate the cheese for the sauce and topping.

3 Heat the butter or margarine in a pan, stir in the flour, then gradually blend in the milk or stock and milk.
4 Bring to the boil and stir until thickened, add the chicken and the 100 g/4 oz grated cheese and season to taste. Add the drained macaroni and spoon into a flameproof dish.
5 Top with the remainder of the grated cheese, the breadcrumbs and small pieces of butter or margarine and brown under the grill for a few minutes.

Note:

If preferred, the chicken and macaroni mixture can be put into an ovenproof dish and placed just above the centre of a moderately hot oven (190°C, 375°F, Gas Mark 5) for 25–30 minutes.

Chicken and macaroni Milanaise

you will need for 4 servings:

METRIC/IMPERIAL

2–3 sticks celery	salt and pepper
4 joints frying chicken	100 g/4 oz quick-cooking
600 ml/1 pint water	macaroni
1 (397-g/14-oz) can tomatoes or 450 g/1 lb tomatoes plus an extra 150 ml/¼ pint water	

to garnish:

50 g/2 oz grated cheese	chopped parsley

1 Cut the celery into 2·5-cm/1-inch pieces.
2 Put the celery, chicken, water and tomatoes plus the liquid from the can into a large saucepan. If using fresh tomatoes, skin them first.
3 Bring the liquid to the boil; add the seasoning then cover the pan, lower the heat and simmer gently for 20 minutes.
4 Add the macaroni and continue cooking a little more rapidly for 10 minutes until the macaroni and chicken are tender. (Do not try to drain the macaroni.)
5 Spoon into a heated dish and top with grated cheese and chopped parsley.

Lasagne alla cacciatora

If lasagne, the long wide ribbon noodle, is not available, use ordinary noodles.

you will need for 4–6 servings:

METRIC/IMPERIAL

for the sauce:

1 large onion	150 ml/¼ pint water
1–2 cloves garlic	150 ml/¼ pint red wine
4–5 large tomatoes	salt and pepper
2–3 rashers bacon	1 teaspoon chopped fresh or pinch dried oregano
75 g/3 oz butter	1 teaspoon chopped fresh or pinch dried basil
1 tablespoon oil	
4 joints young chicken	
175–225 g/6–8 oz plain or green lasagne	100 g/4 oz Parmesan cheese

1 Prepare the sauce first as it takes longer than the pasta (although lasagne is improved with time to drain and dry after cooking). Peel and chop the onion and garlic; skin and slice the tomatoes and dice the bacon.
2 Heat two-thirds of the butter with the oil and fry the onion, garlic and bacon until golden; add the chicken joints and heat for 2–3 minutes. Put in the tomatoes, water, wine, seasoning and herbs.
3 Cover the pan and simmer for about 15 minutes until the chicken is just tender; remove the chicken.
4 Cut the chicken flesh into bite-size pieces, return to the pan and cook uncovered for 2–3 minutes for any surplus liquid to evaporate; the sauce should be the consistency of a thin purée.
5 Meanwhile cook the lasagne in 2·25 litres/4 pints of salted water until tender, drain and dry. Cut into convenient size pieces.
6 Grate the cheese then put a layer of pasta, half the chicken mixture and about one-third of the grated cheese into an ovenproof dish; top with another layer of lasagne, the rest of the chicken sauce and half the remaining cheese.
7 Top with lasagne, the last of the cheese and last one-third of the butter, melted. Heat through in the centre of a moderately hot oven (190°C, 375°F, Gas Mark 5), for about 15–20 minutes.

Note:
This particular pasta has a great advantage for freezing. If you prepare the dish with a cheese *as well as* the chicken sauce (below) you do not need to pre-cook the lasagne. The heating after freezing softens it sufficiently.

Variation:
For a moister dish, make a cheese sauce (see page 41) using 25 g/1 oz butter or margarine, etc., and 300 ml/½ pint milk; add this sauce as an extra layer to the lasagne and chicken mixture. The Parmesan cheese can be omitted or some added to the cheese sauce for a stronger taste.

Cannelloni alla cacciatora

Cannelloni is the tube shaped pasta. If unavailable, make small pancakes (see page 88).

you will need for 4–6 servings:

METRIC/IMPERIAL
225 g/8 oz cannelloni   salt

for the filling:

4 joints young chicken	50 g/2 oz butter or 2
2 onions	tablespoons oil
1–2 cloves garlic	½ teaspoon chopped fresh
3 tomatoes	or generous pinch dried oregano

for the sauce:

40 g/1½ oz butter or margarine	300 ml/½ pint milk
40 g/1½ oz flour	50–75 g/2–3 oz Parmesan cheese
150 ml/¼ pint chicken stock	2 tablespoons double cream

1 Cook the cannelloni in about 2·25 litres/4 pints of boiling salted water until just soft; lift out and drain well.
2 Meanwhile cook the chicken in a little salted water until tender then remove the meat from the bones (the bones could be returned to the liquid and simmered to provide a stronger stock for the sauce).
3 Peel and chop the onions and garlic and skin and slice the tomatoes.
4 Heat the butter or oil and fry the vegetables and garlic until soft; add the chicken, oregano and enough chicken stock to moisten and season well. Fill the cannelloni with this mixture.
5 Make the sauce: heat the butter or margarine, stir in the flour, then gradually add the stock and milk. Bring to the boil and cook until thickened; season well.
6 Pour about half the sauce into an ovenproof dish and add the filled cannelloni. Grate the cheese.
7 Blend the cream and half the cheese into the remaining sauce and spoon over the cannelloni.
8 Heat for about 20 minutes in the centre of a moderately hot oven (190°C, 375°F, Gas Mark 5). Serve with the remaining cheese.

Variations:
Cannelloni with mushroom and liver filling: Slice 100 g/4 oz mushrooms and 175–225 g/6–8 oz chicken livers. Fry in 50–75 g/2–3 oz butter until soft, then moisten with a little chicken stock, tomato purée or red wine and season well. Pound the mixture hard with a wooden spoon so it can be easily inserted into the cannelloni at stage 4. Make the sauce as stage 5.

Cannelloni with cheese and chicken: Make a thick cheese sauce (see page 41) with 25 g/1 oz flour, etc., but using only 150 ml/¼ pint of liquid. Add small pieces of cooked chicken, plus any diced vegetables or leftover stuffing. Fill the cannelloni with this. Make the sauce and proceed as stage 5.

Pies and puddings

Chicken is the basis of many interesting pastry dishes. A traditional chicken pudding is easily made and a splendid choice for a cold day. Party dishes using puff and choux pastry are given in a separate section.

Each recipe gives the pastry most suitable for that particular dish. Where a choice of pastry is given, the one mentioned first seems to me to blend better with the other ingredients. This does not mean you cannot choose the second type or even substitute your own favourite pastry; it may mean, however, that you will need to alter the baking temperatures slightly. If a recipe calls for a topping of shortcrust pastry and you select a richer puff pastry, use a slightly hotter oven at the beginning of the cooking period.

Freezing pastry dishes

The various types of pastry used in these recipes freeze extremely well, either uncooked or after cooking. In fact, it is a wise plan to make batches of pastry (shortcrust, flaky, puff or rough puff) when you have a little spare time, wrap carefully, freeze and use as required. Uncooked pastry keeps for 1 month and should then be used. If the pastry is already cooked as a pie or flan, it will keep in the freezer for up to 3–4 months, but this depends a great deal upon the filling, so it is wiser to use the pies within a shorter period to retain the best flavour. In order to prevent overheating of the pie after freezing, *defrost first*, then either cook as the recipe or reheat gently if it has already been cooked.

Determining amounts

When a recipe states 225 g/8 oz pastry it does not mean the total weight of the pastry, it means pastry made with 225 g/8 oz flour and the other ingredients in proportion. This means that when buying ready-prepared frozen pastry, for 225 g/8 oz home-made shortcrust you buy 350 g/12 oz frozen shortcrust; for 225 g/8 oz home-made puff you buy 450 g/1 lb frozen puff pastry.

When buying pastry mixes, for 225 g/8 oz home-made shortcrust you need 350 g/12 oz shortcrust pastry mix; for 225 g/8 oz home-made flaky you need 350 g/12 oz or a little more flaky pastry mix (the proportion of fat in the pastry mix is not as high as in home-made but it rises well).

Shortcrust pastry

you will need for 4 servings:

METRIC/IMPERIAL
225 g/8 oz plain flour
generous pinch salt

100 g/4 oz fat (see note)

to bind:
water

1 Sift the flour and salt into a basin and rub in the fat until the mixture looks like fine breadcrumbs.
2 Using first a knife and then the fingertips to feel the pastry, gradually add enough cold water to produce a rolling consistency.
3 Lightly flour rolling pin and surface. (If you need a great deal of flour in order to roll out the pastry, you have undoubtedly made it too wet.)
4 Roll out to required thickness and shape, lifting and turning to keep it light.
5 As a general rule, bake in a hot oven (220°C, 425°F, Gas Mark 7); exact cooking times are given in each recipe.

Note:
Use either half butter or margarine and half cooking fat or dripping, all butter, all margarine or all fat. Be generous with metric weights.

Flaky pastry

METRIC/IMPERIAL
225 g/8 oz plain flour
pinch salt
150–175 g/5–6 oz fat (see note)

water
squeeze of lemon juice

1 Sift the flour with the salt.
2 Divide the fat into 3 portions, rub one portion into the flour in the usual way and mix to an elastic consistency with cold water and lemon juice. Roll out to an oblong shape on a lightly floured surface.
3 Divide the second portion of fat into small pieces and lay them on the surface of two-thirds of the dough, leaving the remaining one-third without fat.
4 Fold the uncovered third back over the middle third so that the dough looks like an envelope with its flap open.
5 Fold again over the last third of pastry, so closing the 'envelope'.
6 Turn pastry at right angles, seal the open ends and 'rib' it (depress with the rolling pin at intervals, giving a corrugated effect and equalising the pressure of air).

7 Repeat the rolling and folding process again using the third portion of fat.
8 Roll out pastry once more and, if it feels soft and sticky, leave it in a cold place for 30 minutes.
9 Fold pastry as before, without fat, turn it, seal edges and rib. Altogether the pastry should have 3 rollings and 3 foldings.
10 Stand pastry in a cold place for a short while before baking (the contrast between the cold and the heat of the oven makes the pastry rise better).
11 As a general rule, bake in a hot to very hot oven (230–240°C, 450–475°F, Gas Mark 8–9) for the first 15 minutes, after which the heat can be reduced. Exact cooking times and temperatures are given in each recipe.

Note:
Fat used can be one-third cooking fat and two-thirds margarine, all butter or all margarine.

Variation:
Rough puff pastry: Rub all the fat into the flour and salt at stage 2, then bind with water and lemon juice. Roll out the pastry then give 5 foldings and 5 rollings in all. This is baked like flaky pastry but is a very good substitute for puff pastry.

Puff pastry

METRIC/IMPERIAL
225 g/8 oz plain flour
generous pinch salt
water

squeeze of lemon juice
225 g/8 oz butter

1 Sift the flour and salt together, then mix to an elastic consistency with cold water and lemon juice. Roll out to an oblong shape on a lightly floured surface.
2 Place the butter in the centre of the pastry and fold first the bottom section of pastry over the butter and then the top section so the butter is completely covered.
3 Turn pastry at right angles, seal edges and 'rib' carefully (depress with the rolling pin at intervals) as for flaky pastry.
4 Roll out and fold dough again into an 'envelope' shape.
5 Turn pastry, seal edges, rib and roll again.
6 Repeat 5 times – making 7 rollings and 7 foldings in all – leaving the pastry to rest in a cold place once or twice between rolling to prevent it becoming soft and sticky. Cool thoroughly before rolling for the last time and before baking.
7 As a general rule bake for the first 10–15 minutes in a very hot oven (240°C, 475°F, Gas Mark 9) after which the heat can be reduced. Exact cooking times and temperatures are given in each recipe.

Note:
Well made puff pastry should rise to 4–5 times its original thickness.

Hot water crust pastry

This pastry is used for raised pies.

you will need for 4 servings:
METRIC/IMPERIAL
350 g/12 oz plain flour
pinch salt
150 ml/¼ pint water

100 g/4 oz cooking fat, lard or dripping

1 Sift the flour and salt together.
2 Put the water and fat into a pan and heat only until the fat has melted; pour over the flour.
3 Mix with a knife then knead gently with the fingers. Unlike other pastry, the dough should be kept warm.
4 As a general rule, bake in a moderate oven (180°C, 350°F, Gas Mark 4); exact cooking times and temperatures are given in each recipe.

Suet crust pastry

METRIC/IMPERIAL
225 g/8 oz self-raising flour
generous pinch salt

110 g/4 oz shredded suet
water to bind

1 Sift the flour (or plain flour and 2 teaspoons baking powder) with the salt.
2 Add the suet and enough water and mix to make a fairly elastic dough.
3 Exact cooking times and temperatures are given in each recipe.

Celery and chicken pie

you will need for 6 servings:
METRIC/IMPERIAL
50 g/2 oz chicken fat or butter
25 g/1 oz flour
150 ml/¼ pint chicken stock
150 ml/¼ pint milk
50–100 g/2–4 oz mushrooms

450 g/1 lb cooked chicken
1 small canned or cooked celery heart
salt and pepper
shortcrust pastry made with 350 g/12 oz flour (see page 59)

to glaze:
1 egg or a little milk

1 Make a sauce with half of the fat or butter, the flour, chicken stock and milk.
2 Slice the mushrooms and fry in the remaining fat or butter; blend with the sauce.
3 Dice the chicken; drain then chop the celery heart neatly and mix both ingredients with the sauce. Season well and allow to cool.
4 Roll out the pastry and use nearly two-thirds to line a 20–23-cm/8–9-inch fairly deep pie plate or flan dish.
5 Fill with the chicken mixture, damp the edges of the pastry with cold water, cover with the remaining pastry and seal the edges.

6 Brush the top with beaten egg or a little milk, knock up edges with the back of a knife and decorate.

7 Bake in the centre of a hot oven (220°C, 425°F, Gas Mark 7) for 10–15 minutes, then reduce the heat to moderate (180°C, 350°F, Gas Mark 4) and cook for a further 20–25 minutes until the pastry is crisp and golden. Serve hot.

Variations:

Garden chicken pie: Omit the mushrooms and celery. Substitute 100 g/4 oz cooked peas and 225 g/8 oz mixed grated raw carrots, turnips, swedes and potatoes at stage 3. Add 1 tablespoon chopped parsley, ½ teaspoon chopped rosemary and 2 table-spoons grated raw onion. (The root vegetables could be diced and partly cooked instead of grated if preferred.)

Onion and chicken pie: Omit the mushrooms and celery. Peel and slice 3 large onions and fry in 25–50 g/1–2 oz chicken fat or butter until just tender. Blend with the sauce at stage 3.

Cornish chicken pasties

These are excellent with chicken instead of steak.

you will need for 4 servings:

METRIC/IMPERIAL	
shortcrust pastry made with 350 g/12 oz flour (see page 59)	2 large potatoes
	2 onions
	2 tablespoons chicken stock
225 g/8 oz raw young chicken	salt and pepper
to glaze:	
1 egg	water

1 Roll out the pastry and cut into 4 large rounds (you may need to cut round a small tea plate).

2 Cut the chicken into 5-mm–1-cm/¼–½-inch dice; peel and dice the potatoes and onions. Mix with the chicken, chicken stock and seasoning.

3 Spoon the mixture into the centre of each pastry round; moisten the edges, seal then flute into pasty shapes. Place on a greased baking tray.

4 Beat the egg with a few drops of water and brush over the pasties. Bake for 15 minutes in the centre of a hot oven (220°C, 425°F, Gas Mark 7) then reduce the heat to moderate (160°C, 325°F, Gas Mark 3) for a further 40 minutes. Serve hot or cold.

Giblet, egg and bacon pie

you will need for 2–4 servings:

METRIC/IMPERIAL	
chicken giblets	2 hard-boiled eggs
salt and pepper	shortcrust pastry made with 225 g/8 oz flour (see page 59)
15 g/½ oz flour	
100 g/4 oz lean bacon	
to glaze:	
1 egg or a little milk	

1 Simmer the giblets until tender, then strain off nearly all the stock, reserving about 2 tablespoons.

2 Cut all the meat from the neck of the chicken; chop liver, heart and kidney finely and dust lightly with well seasoned flour; dice the bacon and slice the eggs.

3 Roll out the pastry and line a pie plate or sandwich tin with half of it.

4 Cover the pastry with half the giblet meat then the sliced hard-boiled eggs and bacon.

5 Add the reserved stock and cover with the remaining giblet meat. Damp the edges of the pastry.

6 Put the rest of the pastry over the top, seal the edges and decorate with leaves of pastry.

7 Brush with a little beaten egg or milk and bake in the centre of a hot oven (220°C, 425°F, Gas Mark 7) for about 20 minutes, then lower heat to moderate (180°C, 350°F, Gas Mark 4) for a further 20 minutes; serve hot or cold.

Variations:

Giblet and mushroom pie: Substitute 100–175 g/4–6 oz sliced mushrooms for the hard-boiled eggs at stage 4.

Giblet and onion pie: Substitute 4 boiled, chopped onions for the hard-boiled eggs at stage 4.

Giblet pasties: Increase the amount of pastry to that made with 275–350 g/10–12 oz flour, roll out and cut into 4 large rounds. Make the filling or any of the variations and put the filling in the centre of each round of pastry. Bake first for 15 minutes, then lower the heat for a further 10–15 minutes at stage 7.

Giblet and rice pie: This is an excellent way of making a more substantial dish from the giblets. First cook 50 g/2 oz long-grain rice; it can be cooked in chicken stock to give it more flavour. Add 2 chopped onions to the rice while it cooks then place in the pie dish at stage 4. Because you have rather more filling you will need pastry made with 275 g/10 oz flour.

Curried chicken pie: Blend 2 teaspoons curry powder with the flour at stage 2 and add 100 g/4 oz cooked and diced chicken to the giblets at stage 2.

Chicken pie (1)

you will need for 4–6 servings:

METRIC/IMPERIAL	
1 small chicken	strip of lemon rind
water to cover	2 eggs
salt and pepper	2–3 rashers bacon
1 teaspoon chopped fresh or pinch dried mixed herbs	shortcrust pastry made with 175–225 g/6–8 oz flour (see page 59)

1 Simmer the chicken in water to cover until just tender with the giblets, seasoning, mixed herbs and the grated or thinly pared lemon rind.

2 Lift the chicken and giblets from the stock and dice neatly; the giblet meat could be omitted if desired,

but it gives flavour to the pie. Blend the light and dark meat together.

3 Boil the chicken stock steadily to reduce it so it becomes stronger in flavour; hard-boil the eggs.

4 Chop the uncooked bacon into small pieces and slice the hard-boiled eggs.

5 Season the meat well and put a layer of chicken meat, then egg then bacon into a pie dish.

6 Repeat until the pie dish is full, then add approximately 300 ml/½ pint of the strained reduced chicken stock; do not over-fill the dish with liquid.

7 Roll out the pastry, cover the filling and bake in the centre of a hot oven (220°C, 425°F, Gas Mark 7) for approximately 15 minutes, until the pastry becomes pale golden, then lower the heat to moderate (180°C, 350°F, Gas Mark 4) for a further 25–30 minutes; serve hot or cold.

Note:

The pastry can be glazed with beaten egg at stage 7 before baking.

Variations:

Chicken pie (2): Omit the giblets for a milder stock. Omit the eggs and bacon. Put all the diced chicken into a pie dish. Measure out 300 ml/½ pint of the chicken stock and make a coating sauce with 25 g/ 1 oz chicken fat or butter, 25 g/1 oz flour and the stock. Pour over the chicken and proceed as stage 7.

Chicken and vegetable pie: Add lightly cooked root vegetables to the diced chicken at stage 2.

Creamed chicken pie: At stage 6, use a little less stock and blend with single cream to make up to 300 ml/½ pint.

Swiss cheese and chicken pie

Shortcrust is better than flaky or puff pastry for flans, as it keeps a better shape. This flan may be made in advance and reheated.

you will need for 4–6 servings:
METRIC/IMPERIAL

175 g/6 oz Gruyère cheese	15 g/½ oz flour
175–225 g/6–8 oz cooked chicken	3 eggs
shortcrust pastry made with 175 g/6 oz flour (see page 59)	150 ml/¼ pint milk or single cream
	salt and pepper

1 Grate the cheese; cut the chicken into small pieces. Mix the cheese with the chicken.

2 Roll out the pastry thinly on a lightly floured surface and line a 23-cm/9-inch flan tin.

3 Dredge the cheese and chicken mixture with the flour and distribute evenly over the base of the flan case.

4 Beat the eggs, mix with the milk or cream and season lightly. Pour over the cheese and chicken mixture and bake for 15 minutes in a hot oven (220°C, 425°F, Gas Mark 7).

5 Reduce heat to cool (150°C, 300°F, Gas Mark 2) and bake for a further 30 minutes or until the pastry is crisp and the filling firm; serve warm.

Variations:

Chicken quiche: Use Gruyère cheese or substitute grated Cheddar. Grill or fry 2–3 rashers lean bacon, chop and add to the cheese and chicken mixture at stage 3; omit the flour.

Chicken and vegetable quiche: Add 100 g/4 oz cooked sliced mushrooms and/or diced canned red pepper and cooked peas to the chicken and cheese mixture at stage 3; omit the flour.

To bake blind

If a recipe calls for pastry to be baked blind, roll out the pastry and put it into the flan dish, or a flan ring on an upturned baking tray (this makes it easier to remove after baking). To prevent the bottom pastry rising in baking and the sides losing their shape, put greased foil greased side down on to the pastry and press down firmly, or place greased greaseproof paper on the pastry and weight it down with dried beans, crusts of bread or macaroni. Bake for about 15 minutes in the centre of a hot oven (220°C, 425°F, Gas Mark 7) until the pastry begins to turn golden brown, then remove the foil or paper. Finish cooking the flan according to the recipe. The flan ring can be removed for the last minute of baking to make sure the sides are well cooked.

Chicken cream pasty

you will need for 3–4 servings:
METRIC/IMPERIAL

1–2 eggs	½ teaspoon finely grated lemon rind
shortcrust or flaky pastry made with 175 g/6 oz flour (see pages 59, 60)	1 teaspoon chopped parsley
350 g/12 oz cooked chicken	1 tablespoon fine soft breadcrumbs
2 tablespoons cream	salt and pepper

to glaze:
1 egg or a little milk

1 Hard-boil the egg(s), cool and chop neatly.

2 Roll out the pastry into a large square.

3 Dice the chicken, blend with the egg, cream, lemon rind, parsley, breadcrumbs and seasoning; put in the centre of the pastry.

4 Bring up the 4 corners of the pastry into the centre, brushing them with a little egg or milk to seal; lift on to a greased baking tray.

5 Decorate with a rose of pastry and brush with more beaten egg or milk.

6 Bake in the centre of a moderately hot oven (200°C, 400°F, Gas Mark 6) if using shortcrust pastry, or a hot oven (220°C, 425°F, Gas Mark 7), for flaky pastry, for 15–20 minutes, then lower heat to moderate (180°C, 350°F, Gas Mark 4) for a further 10

minutes until the pastry is firm; serve hot or cold.

Variation:
Chicken rice pasty: Substitute 25 g/1 oz cooked rice for the breadcrumbs and flavour with 2 tablespoons chopped chives at stage 3.

Chicken and mushroom pie

you will need for 4–6 servings:

METRIC/IMPERIAL	
1 young chicken	salt and pepper
2 onions	300 ml/½ pint chicken
2 tomatoes	stock
100 g/4 oz mushrooms	flaky pastry made with
75 g/3 oz fat bacon	175 g/6 oz flour (see
25 g/1 oz flour	page 59)
generous pinch thyme	

to glaze:
1 egg

1 Cut the chicken into neat joints (remove the bones if desired).
2 Peel and chop the onions, peel and slice the tomatoes, slice the mushrooms and dice the bacon.
3 Heat the bacon in a pan then lift the bacon out of the pan and fry the chopped onions, sliced tomatoes and mushrooms in the fat remaining, adding an extra knob of dripping or fat if necessary.
4 Roll the jointed chicken in the flour and toss in the fat to brown, then place in a pie dish with the vegetables, bacon and thyme and season to taste.
5 Heat the stock in the pan, stirring to absorb any fat and flour remaining, then pour about 150 ml/¼ pint into the pie dish; reserve the remainder for a sauce to serve with the pie.
6 Cover the dish with pastry, brush with beaten egg and bake for approximately 15 minutes in the centre of a hot oven (230°C, 450°F, Gas Mark 8).
7 Reduce heat to moderately hot (190°C, 375°F, Gas Mark 5) and cook for a further 1 hour at least, covering the pastry with greaseproof paper so that it does not overbrown.

Variations:
Chicken and tomato pie: Omit the mushrooms and use 6–8 tomatoes.

Jellied chicken pie: Omit the mushrooms and tomatoes. Simmer a pig's trotter with the bones of the chicken to give the kind of stock that will form a jelly when cold. Allow to simmer until reduced to just 300 ml/½ pint. Cool then skim off the surplus fat. Blend with the jointed chicken. Omit the flour, but season well and add the herbs. Put the chicken and bacon mixture into the pie dish with as much of the stock as the dish will hold. Continue as stages 6 and 7 and allow to cool. Serve with salad.

Chicken and bacon pie

In this recipe the uncooked chicken is used.

you will need for 6 servings:

METRIC/IMPERIAL	
1 young chicken	6 bacon rashers
salt and pepper	2 onions
flaky or puff pastry made	3 tomatoes
with 175 g/6 oz flour	chicken stock
(see pages 59, 60)	

1 Cut the meat from the bones of the chicken, then cover the chicken bones with water, add seasoning and simmer for at least 1 hour, or allow 30 minutes at High (15 lb) pressure. In order to give a more concentrated stock you can then boil steadily in an open pan until reduced to about 300 ml/½ pint; cool.
2 Put the pastry in the refrigerator to cool. Chop the bacon, peel and chop the onions and tomatoes.
3 Put a layer of the chicken meat into a pie dish (the diced raw liver from the giblets could be added if desired).
4 Cover with a layer of chopped bacon, onion and tomatoes. Fill the dish, alternating layers and moistening the layers of chicken with the stock made from the chicken bones; add extra seasoning if required.
5 Roll out the pastry on a lightly floured surface. Cover the filling with the pastry and bake for approximately 15 minutes in the centre of a hot oven (230°C, 450°F, Gas Mark 8) then reduce heat to moderate (160°C, 325°F, Gas Mark 3). Cook for a further 1 hour at least, covering the pastry with greaseproof paper or foil so it does not overbrown.

Variation:
Chicken, bacon and egg pie: Omit the onions and tomatoes. Mix together the diced raw chicken and diced bacon. Put into a pie dish, cover with the stock then break 4–6 eggs carefully over the filling, or if preferred, hard-boil 4–6 eggs and put in the centre of the bacon and chicken mixture. Cover with the pastry and bake as at stage 5.

Chicken and ham pie

you will need for 4 servings:

METRIC/IMPERIAL	
2 eggs	salt and pepper
hot water crust pastry,	1–2 teaspoons grated
made with 350 g/12 oz	lemon rind
flour (see page 60)	3 tablespoons chicken
175 g/6 oz ham	stock
700 g/1½ lb boned	
uncooked chicken	

to glaze:	
1 egg	4 tablespoons chicken
1 teaspoon gelatine	stock

1 Hard-boil the eggs, shell and keep whole. Keep the pastry warm in a basin until ready to use.

2 Use two-thirds of the pastry to line a 15–18-cm/6–7-inch round cake tin or a 750-g/1½-lb loaf tin, or mould into desired shape (see note).
3 Cut the ham and chicken into 2·5-cm/1-inch cubes and roll in seasoning and lemon rind.
4 Place half the meat in the bottom of the pastry-lined tin or shape, place the eggs on top of the meat and cover with remaining meat.
5 Pour the 3 tablespoons of chicken stock over the filling. Turn the top edges of the pastry lining in over the meat and damp with cold water.
6 Roll out the remaining one-third of pastry to make a lid and press down all round the edge.
7 Make a hole in the centre, brush the top with beaten egg and decorate with pastry leaves and a rose; once again brush with beaten egg.
8 Place in the centre of a moderate oven (180°C, 350°F, Gas Mark 4) and cook for 2–2¼ hours. Leave to cool.
9 Melt the gelatine in the 4 tablespoons stock; when the pie is cool and the gelatine mixture just setting, pour into the pie through the hole in the centre. Leave to set before serving.

To shape a raised pie

There are two ways of shaping a raised pie: in the first you need a tin in which to bake the pie, so the pastry should be rolled out then cut into two shapes (the same size as the bottom of the tin) for the bottom and the top of the pie, then a long strip to go round the sides of the tin. Put in the bottom shape, moisten the edges; press the strip along the bottom and the inside of the tin. Add the filling, moisten the top edge of the long strip then place the lid in position. Continue as stage 7.

In the second method you do not need to roll out the pastry, but mould two-thirds of it round the outside of a tin or other shape, giving the base and sides. Remove the tin, add the filling, then press or roll out the pastry for the lid, press down round the edge and proceed as stage 7.

Suet puddings

The golden rule for a light suet pudding is to make sure the water boils rapidly for the first half of the cooking period. If you prefer a thicker, well risen crust use self-raising flour, or plain flour plus baking powder. For a thinner crust which does not rise in cooking use plain flour and no raising agent.

You will need to cook the pudding for at least 2½ hours so that the crust is light, so this is a case when it is better to choose an older fowl, as a young bird tends to be overcooked in that time.

Using a pressure cooker

If you own a pressure cooker, check the directions for steaming puddings for a period and then cooking under pressure in your particular model (this saves an appreciable amount of cooking time). In most pressure cookers you will need to put at least 750 ml/1¼ pints water into the pan with the trivet, steam the pudding without pressure for 15 minutes then bring up to Low (5 lb) pressure, lower the heat and cook for 55 minutes.

Chicken pudding

you will need for 6 servings:

METRIC/IMPERIAL
1 boiling fowl	salt and pepper
50–100 g/2–4 oz bacon	150 ml/¼ pint chicken
1 onion	stock or water
suet crust pastry made with 275–350 g/10–12 oz flour (see page 60)	

1 Joint the chicken, remove the bones if possible and cut the chicken flesh and bacon into neat pieces; peel and dice the onion.
2 Roll out the pastry and use three-quarters to line a greased 1·25–1·5-litre/2–2½-pint basin.
3 Add the chicken, bacon, onion, seasoning and the liquid. Cover with a lid made from the last quarter of pastry, greased greaseproof paper and foil.
4 Steam over boiling water for 3½–4 hours and serve with thickened gravy.

Note:
For a richer liquid coat the chicken pieces in seasoned flour at stage 1.

Variations:
Chicken and leek pudding: Omit the bacon and substitute 3–4 chopped leeks.

Chicken and ham pudding: Omit the bacon and substitute 100 g/4 oz chopped cooked or (preferably) raw ham.

Chicken and mushroom pudding: Omit the bacon and substitute 100 g/4 oz small mushrooms.

Chicken and vegetable pudding: Omit the bacon and substitute approximately 225 g/8 oz diced uncooked vegetables.

Special occasion dishes

The following recipes are selected for special occasions: some for when you are short of time, others for buffet parties and finally recipes based on dishes from other countries.

Chicken in white wine and mushroom sauce

you will need for 4 servings:

METRIC/IMPERIAL

4 joints young chicken	150 ml/$\frac{1}{4}$ pint water
150 ml/$\frac{1}{4}$ pint white wine	salt and pepper

for the sauce:

50 g/2 oz mushrooms	25 g/1 oz flour
50 g/2 oz butter or margarine	150 ml/$\frac{1}{4}$ pint milk

to garnish:
chopped parsley

1 Put the chicken joints into a greased casserole and pour over the wine and water; add seasoning and cover.
2 Bake in the centre of a moderately hot oven (200°C, 400°F, Gas Mark 6) for 30 minutes.
3 Prepare the sauce: chop the mushrooms then heat the butter or margarine and fry the mushrooms until just soft.
4 Blend in the flour, then gradually add the milk and stir over a low heat until very thick.
5 Lift the chicken on to a warm dish, strain the liquid into the sauce and reheat without boiling. Pour over the chicken and garnish with parsley.

Note:
To freeze, prepare to stage 4. Use very little wine and add extra wine when reheating. Complete the sauce and serve.

Chicken in mushroom and tomato sauce

you will need for 4 servings:

METRIC/IMPERIAL

50 g/2 oz butter or margarine	150 ml/$\frac{1}{4}$ pint Burgundy
	salt and pepper
4 joints frying chicken	4 tablespoons chicken
100 g/4 oz mushrooms	stock
1 large onion	25 g/1 oz flour
225 g/8 oz tomatoes	

1 Heat the butter or margarine in a large pan and fry the chicken joints until pale golden on both sides then place in a casserole.

2 Slice the mushrooms, peel and chop the onion and skin and halve the tomatoes.
3 Add the sliced mushrooms and 1 teaspoon chopped onion to the chicken.
4 Pour the Burgundy over the chicken mixture and season well. Cook for 20 minutes in the centre of a moderate oven (180°C, 350°F, Gas Mark 4).
5 Prepare the sauce: put the tomatoes and stock into a saucepan with the remaining onion and more seasoning. Simmer until just soft then sieve or liquidise. Blend the flour with the tomato purée.
6 Put the chicken joints on to a warm dish, add the liquid and mushrooms from the casserole to the tomato purée and stir over a moderate heat until thickened. Coat the chicken with the sauce.

Note:
This dish is not suitable for freezing.

Variation:
Use stock plus 1 tablespoon red wine vinegar instead of Burgundy at stage 4.

Chicken with almonds

you will need for 4 servings:

METRIC/IMPERIAL

4 tablespoons oil	450 ml/$\frac{3}{4}$ pint chicken
25 g/1 oz butter	stock
2 onions	50 g/2 oz blanched
3 tomatoes	almonds
4 joints young chicken	50 g/2 oz sultanas
salt and pepper	100–175 g/4–6 oz long-
pinch ground cinnamon	grain rice

to garnish:
finely chopped parsley

1 Heat the oil and butter in a pan.
2 Peel and thinly slice the onions, skin and de-seed the tomatoes and cut into thin shreds.
3 Put the chicken joints in the pan and fry on both sides then place in a casserole.
4 Add the onions and tomatoes to the fat remaining in the pan, fry for a few minutes then add to the chicken.
5 Season well and add a pinch of cinnamon.
6 Pour over the stock, cover and cook in the centre of a moderate oven (180°C, 350°F, Gas Mark 4) for 40 minutes. After 20 minutes add the almonds and sultanas.
7 Meanwhile cook the rice. Serve the chicken with a border of boiled rice and garnish with chopped parsley.

Note:
This dish is not suitable for freezing.

Spiced chicken with cherries

you will need for 4–6 servings:

METRIC/IMPERIAL

4–6 joints young chicken	25 g/1 oz flour
paprika and salt	1 teaspoon sugar
1 (425-g/15-oz) can red	¼ teaspoon ground cloves
cherries	¼ teaspoon ground
1 (226-g/8 oz) can	cinnamon
crushed pineapple	⅛ teaspoon dry mustard
chicken stock (if	2 tablespoons rum or ½
necessary)	chicken stock cube plus
50–75 g/2–3 oz butter	2 tablespoons water

1 Season the chicken joints with paprika and salt.
2 Drain and stone the cherries if necessary, reserving the syrup. Drain the pineapple: if crushed pineapple is not available, finely chop pineapple rings or cubes.
3 Measure the combined fruit syrups. If necessary dilute with a little chicken stock to make up to 450 ml/¾ pint.
4 Heat the butter in the pan and fry the chicken joints until golden; lift on to a plate.
5 Blend the flour, sugar, spices and mustard into the butter remaining in the pan then add the fruit syrup; bring to the boil and cook until smooth and thickened.
6 Add the rum or the stock cube and water (the latter gives a more definite taste) together with the chicken joints.
7 Cover the pan and simmer for 20–30 minutes until the chicken is just tender, then add the cherries and pineapple and heat through for 5 minutes.

Note:
If preferred the dish may be prepared to stage 7 then cooked in a covered casserole for 25–35 minutes in the centre of a moderately hot oven (190°C, 375°F, Gas Mark 5). Add the fruit towards the end of the cooking time. To freeze, add the rum when reheating.

Chicken in sour cream sauce

you will need for 4 servings:

METRIC/IMPERIAL

1 onion	salt and pepper
100-g/4-oz piece lean	300 ml/½ pint chicken
bacon	stock
2 small spring chickens	1 bay leaf
100 g/4 oz button	small piece lemon rind
mushrooms	150 ml/¼ pint Marsala or
25 g/1 oz butter	claret
1 tablespoon chopped	
parsley	

for the sauce:

25 g/1 oz butter	150 ml/¼ pint soured
25 g/1 oz flour	cream (or single cream
	plus 1 tablespoon lemon
	juice)

1 Peel and chop the onion and dice the bacon; halve the chickens; wipe but do not peel the mushrooms.

2 Heat the butter and fry the bacon, onion and mushrooms for several minutes; blend in the parsley.
3 Place in a casserole with the chicken halves on top. Season the stock and pour over the chickens; add the bay leaf, lemon rind and wine.
4 Cover the casserole and cook in a moderate oven (180°C, 350°F, Gas Mark 4) for 40 minutes or until tender. Lift the chicken on to a warm dish and keep warm.
5 Heat the butter for the sauce in a pan, stir in the flour and add the liquid, bacon and vegetables from the casserole; remove the bay leaf.
6 Bring to the boil, lower the heat and simmer for 5 minutes, then remove from the heat and add the soured cream or fresh cream and lemon juice.
7 Heat gently but do not boil; spoon over the chicken.

Note:
To freeze, prepare to stage 6 and stir in the soured cream when reheating.

Chicken in mushroom sauce

you will need for 4 servings:

METRIC/IMPERIAL

2 spring chickens	100–225 g/4–8 oz button
salt and pepper	mushrooms
25 g/1 oz flour	300 ml/½ pint milk
50 g/2 oz butter or	2 tablespoons Burgundy
margarine	or port wine

to garnish:

paprika	chopped parsley

1 Cut the chickens into halves through the breast.
2 Mix seasoning with half the flour and roll the chickens in it.
3 Heat the butter or margarine in a pan and toss the chicken in it until the flour is a very pale brown then put into a casserole.
4 Wash the mushrooms and chop half of them but keep the rest whole.
5 Toss the chopped mushrooms in any butter or margarine remaining in the pan (if necessary add a little extra).
6 Blend in the remaining flour then add the milk; bring to the boil and cook until the sauce has thickened slightly. Remove from the heat and cool slightly.
7 Season well then stir in the wine (do not boil). Arrange the whole mushrooms around the chicken then cover with the sauce.
8 Put a lid on the casserole and bake for 45 minutes in the centre of a moderate oven (160°C, 325°F, Gas Mark 3). Serve garnished with paprika and chopped parsley.

Note:
To freeze, add the wine when reheating.

Variation:
Chicken soubise: Omit the mushrooms and substitute 3 onions. Peel the onions and cut into thin rings. Fry

all the onions at stage 5 until transparent and tender. You may need to add an extra 25 g/1 oz butter or margarine.

Chicken Newburg

you will need for 4 servings:

METRIC/IMPERIAL

450–750 g/1–1½ lb cooked chicken	150 ml/¼ pint sherry
50 g/2 oz butter	150 ml/¼ pint cream
½ teaspoon paprika	2 egg yolks
salt and pepper	300 ml/½ pint milk

1 Divide the chicken into neat pieces.
2 Heat the butter in the top of a double saucepan, put in the chicken pieces and turn them in the butter for 3–4 minutes. Season with paprika, salt and pepper.
3 Pour in the sherry and simmer gently for 10 minutes.
4 Stir in the cream and blend well.
5 Add the egg yolks, thoroughly beaten with the milk, just before serving.
6 Stir over a gentle heat without letting the sauce come to the boil, until creamy. Serve with plain boiled rice.

Note:
This dish is not suitable for freezing.

Choux pastry

you will need for 4 servings:

METRIC/IMPERIAL

150 ml/¼ pint water	75 g/3 oz plain or self-raising flour
25 g/1 oz butter or margarine	2 eggs and 1 egg yolk or 3 small eggs
salt and pepper	

1 Put the water and butter or margarine into a saucepan and heat until the fat has melted.
2 Sift the seasoning with the flour. Remove the pan from the heat and stir in the seasoned flour.
3 Return to a low heat and cook very gently, stirring all the time, until the mixture is dry enough to form a ball and leave the pan clean.
4 Remove from the heat once again and gradually add the well beaten eggs (you may find you do not need all of the third yolk or egg). The mixture should be sticky enough to stand in peaks but sufficiently soft to pipe into shapes.

Shaping choux pastry

Put the mixture into a piping bag or spoon as follows:

Choux: Make into round bun shapes. Bake for 25–30 minutes just above the centre of a moderately hot oven (190–200°C, 375–400°F, Gas Mark 5–6), reducing the heat after about 20 minutes. When cooked, split and remove any uncooked mixture then dry out in the oven for a few minutes before filling.

Eclairs: Make into finger shapes and bake as for choux, allowing only about 20 minutes of cooking time.

Profiteroles: Make into small rounds the size of a hazelnut (they will puff up larger in cooking). Bake as for choux but allow only 10–12 minutes of cooking time.

Note:
If desired, bake, cool then freeze or put in cold filling and freeze.

Chicken choux

you will need for 6 servings:

METRIC/IMPERIAL

choux pastry made with 75 g/3 oz flour (see page 67)	225–350 g/8–12 oz cooked chicken

for the sauce:

25 g/1 oz butter or margarine	salt and pepper
25 g/1 oz flour	1–2 tablespoons double cream or mayonnaise
200–300 ml/⅓–½ pint milk or milk and chicken stock	

1 Either put the choux pastry into a piping bag with a 1–2·5-cm/½–1-inch plain nozzle and pipe into bun shapes on a greased baking tray, or alternatively put spoonfuls of the mixture on a greased baking tray or in greased patty tins. Whichever method is used, space well apart to allow the pastry to rise.
2 Bake as for the desired shape (see above).
3 Prepare the filling. Mince or dice the chicken and make a white sauce (see page 41), using the smaller amount of liquid if serving the choux as a hot savoury; whip the cream if used.
4 Add the chicken to the sauce with the cream or mayonnaise.
5 To serve hot, fill hot choux buns with hot mixture and serve immediately. To serve cold, allow both choux buns and chicken mixture to cool before filling.

Variations:
Chicken éclairs: Make and bake as described (see page 67). Fill with the chicken mixture. Dip each end in thick mayonnaise then finely chopped herbs or chopped nuts just before serving. Makes 10–18 depending on size.

Chicken profiteroles: Make and bake as described (see page 67). Fill with the chicken mixture. Serve hot or cold as a cocktail savoury. Makes about 24.

Vol-au-vent cases (1)

you will need for 4 servings:

METRIC/IMPERIAL
puff pastry made with
  225 g/8 oz flour (see
  page 60)

to glaze:
I egg

1 Roll out the puff pastry until just under 1 cm/½ inch thick then cut into 8 rounds.
2 From half the rounds make a ring by cutting out the centre. Place each ring on top of a complete round; be careful not to stretch the pastry.
3 Seal edges and put on *damp* baking trays.
4 Glaze with beaten egg; chill before baking.
5 Bake just above or in the centre of a hot to very hot oven (230–240°C, 450–475°F, Gas Mark 8–9) until well risen and brown, about 12–15 minutes, then reduce heat slightly to make sure the pastry is cooked.

Note:

This method can be used for shapes other than rounds, although it is more difficult to make a good squared rim. These shapes are easier made by method 2 (see below).

Vol-au-vent cases (2)

you will need for 4 servings:

METRIC/IMPERIAL
puff pastry made with
  225 g/8 oz flour (see
  page 60)

to glaze:
I egg

1 Roll out the puff pastry until it is 1·5–2·5 cm/¾–1 inch thick, then cut into 4 rounds or required shapes. Put on *damp* baking trays.
2 With a smaller cutter press halfway through the pastry, leaving a 5-mm–1-cm/¼–½-inch rim.
3 Glaze with beaten egg; chill before baking.
4 Bake in a hot to very hot oven (230–240°C, 450–475°F, Gas Mark 8–9) until well risen and brown, about 12–15 minutes, then reduce heat slightly to make sure the pastry is cooked.
5 Lift out the centre portion with the point of a sharp knife and return the cases to the oven for a short time to dry out. (The lids can be placed over the filling.)

Fillings for vol-au-vent cases

Only put the filling in when hot if you want to serve at once or the pastry will be spoilt. When serving *hot* bake the pastry cases and keep them warm. Make the filling, place in the cases and serve at once. When serving *cold* allow both pastry and filling to become cold, then put the filling in the cases and serve.

1 Make a thick béchamel sauce (see page 41) and add diced chicken.
2 Make a Hollandaise sauce (see page 30) and add finely chopped gherkins and diced chicken.
3 Fry a little finely chopped onion and skinned chopped tomatoes; add diced chicken, seasoning and a little chicken stock to moisten. Heat through.
4 Make a thick mushroom sauce (see page 42) and add diced chicken.
5 Make a creamed curry sauce (see page 43), add a little cooked rice and diced chicken and heat.
6 Prepare chicken kedgeree (see page 56), adding the chopped hard-boiled eggs to the rice. If serving cold, blend with 2 tablespoons mayonnaise while the rice mixture is hot, then cool and add the chopped hard-boiled eggs.
7 Make a hard-boiled egg sauce (see page 42), add diced chicken and serve hot. To serve cold, blend a little mayonnaise with the cooled sauce then add the chicken.
8 Make a thick tomato sauce (see page 43) and add diced chicken and diced fried mushrooms.
9 Dice raw tender chicken, fry until tender and mix with cooked vegetables. Bind with a sauce or mayonnaise.
10 Make a barbecue sauce (see page 34) and add enough to moisten minced or diced cooked chicken.
11 Blend cream cheese with a little mayonnaise or cream and diced chicken. Serve cold.
12 Blend mayonnaise with finely diced cucumber, chicken and sliced olives. Serve cold.
13 Make a Tartare sauce (see page 80) and add diced chicken. Serve cold.

Note:

When a thick sauce is called for it means a panada consistency, i.e. 150 ml/¼ pint liquid to each 25 g/1 oz flour if serving the mixture hot. As sauces tend to stiffen as they cool, you could add an extra 1–2 tablespoons liquid if preparing the mixture for a cold filling.

Chicken puffs

you will need for 4–8 servings:

METRIC/IMPERIAL
flaky or puff pastry made
  with 225 g/8 oz flour
  (see pages 59, 60)

for the sauce:

25 g/1 oz butter or margarine	squeeze of lemon juice
25 g/1 oz flour	salt and pepper
150 ml/¼ pint milk	450 g/1 lb cooked chicken
2 tablespoons double cream	sour cream sauce (see page 34)

1 Roll out the pastry to just under 5 mm/¼ inch in

thickness and cut into 8 (10-cm/4-inch) squares.
2 Make a thick white sauce, panada consistency (see page 41), and add the cream, lemon juice and seasoning.
3 Chop the chicken and blend into the sauce; spoon the mixture into the centre of each pastry square.
4 Moisten the edges of the pastry then fold up like an envelope by bringing the corners to the centre; press the joints of the pastry together to seal.
5 Bake in a hot oven (220–230°C, 425–450°F, Gas Mark 7–8) for 10 minutes or until puffed and golden; reduce heat slightly for a further 5 minutes. Serve with sour cream sauce.

Arabian chicken

you will need for 4–6 servings:
METRIC/IMPERIAL

4–6 chicken joints	juice of I orange
salt and pepper	I (312-g/11-oz) can
50 g/2 oz butter	mandarin orange
2 tablespoons honey	segments
2 tablespoons chopped	½ tablespoon cornflour
preserved or crystallised	
ginger	

1 Dry the joints of chicken (if using frozen chicken there is no need to let it thaw out). You can remove the bones from the chicken to make it easier to serve for a buffet.
2 Season lightly and fry in the butter until tender and golden, approximately 15 minutes.
3 Lift the chicken on to a hot dish and keep warm.
4 Stir the honey into the butter remaining in the pan and add seasoning, chopped ginger and orange juice.
5 Drain the juice from the can of mandarin oranges and blend with the cornflour. Tip into the pan with the oranges and continue cooking over a low heat until thickened. Pour over the chicken and serve at once.

Variation:
This dish is a good way to use up leftover cooked chicken. Heat the chicken thoroughly in the hot butter at stage 2, lift from the pan, then proceed as the recipe above.

Chicken bobotie

This is a pleasant adaptation of a traditional South African dish.

you will need for 4–6 servings:
METRIC/IMPERIAL

450 g/I lb cooked chicken	½–I tablespoon lemon
2 large onions	juice
50 g/2 oz chicken fat or	100 g/4 oz soft
butter	breadcrumbs
½–I tablespoon curry	450 ml/¾ pint milk
powder	2 egg yolks
salt and pepper	25–50 g/1–2 oz blanched
I teaspoon sugar	almonds (optional)

1 Cut the chicken into small pieces; peel and chop the onions.
2 Heat the fat or butter in a pan and fry the onions until soft but not coloured.
3 Blend the chicken with the onions, curry powder, seasoning, sugar, lemon juice and breadcrumbs.
4 Moisten with several tablespoons of the milk and put into a large shallow casserole; smooth the top.
5 Heat the remaining milk and add to the beaten egg yolks; season lightly.
6 Pour over the chicken mixture, add the almonds if wished but do not cover the dish.
7 Bake for 45 minutes in the centre of a moderate oven (160°C, 325°F, Gas Mark 3).

Chicken Maryland

you will need for 4 servings:
METRIC/IMPERIAL

4 chicken joints	I egg
salt and pepper	dried breadcrumbs
flour	

to fry:
oil or fat

to garnish:

corn fritters	2 bananas
bacon rolls	watercress

1 Coat the chicken with seasoned flour then egg and breadcrumbs and shallow or deep fry (see pages 23, 24).
2 Make and fry the corn fritters (see recipe below) and cook the bacon rolls (see page 37).
3 Fry the bananas (see note).
4 Drain all the fried foods well on absorbent paper and arrange round the chicken then add the watercress.

Note:
While bananas can be coated with egg and crumbs they are nicer if coated with a little flour and fried in shallow fat until soft.

Variation:
Serve with cooked sweet corn instead of fritters.

Corn fritters

you will need for 4 servings:
METRIC/IMPERIAL

I egg	I (340-g/12-oz) can
2 tablespoons self-raising	sweet corn kernels **or**
flour	225 g/8 oz cooked
salt and cayenne pepper	sweet corn
I teaspoon	
Worcestershire sauce	

to fry:
oil or fat

1 Make a batter with the beaten egg, flour and seasoning. Beat well and mix in the Worcestershire sauce and the drained sweet corn.

2 Gently fry tablespoons of the mixture in a little hot oil or fat, turning once, until golden brown.

Variation:
Make the batter as for chicken fritters (see page 88) and blend the sweet corn with it. The batter can be flavoured with Worcestershire sauce as above.

Chicken Walewska

This combination of poultry and shellfish is unusual but delicious.

you will need for 4 servings:

METRIC/IMPERIAL

1 roasting chicken or 4 joints frying chicken	salt and pepper Hollandaise sauce (see page 30)
150 ml/¼ pint white wine	
meat of 1 small female lobster	lobster butter (see below)

1 Roast or fry the chicken (see pages 35, 23). If roasted, carve or joint the chicken and arrange on a warm dish.
2 Add the white wine, flaked lobster meat and seasoning to the Hollandaise sauce. Heat gently but do not overcook.
3 Pour the sauce over the chicken and top with lobster butter (see below) just before serving.

Lobster butter: Crumble the red coral (roe) of a female lobster then work it into creamed butter. Add a little pepper, lemon juice and a pinch of salt if liked.

Note:
This dish is not suitable for freezing, although Hollandaise sauce can be frozen.

Spring chicken in white wine

you will need for 4 large or 8 small servings:

METRIC/IMPERIAL

100 g/4 oz bacon	2 young chickens
2 onions	6 tablespoons brandy
1 clove garlic	bouquet garni
1 carrot	salt and pepper
100 g/4 oz mushrooms	600 ml/1 pint white wine
75 g/3 oz butter	

for beurre manié:

25 g/1 oz butter	25 g/1 oz flour

1 Dice the bacon, peel and chop the onions and garlic; slice the carrot. Fry the unpeeled mushrooms lightly in the butter then add bacon, onions, garlic and carrot. Remove from the pan.
2 Joint or cut the chickens in half and brown in the butter left in the pan. Add the brandy, ignite and allow to blaze for 1 minute.
3 Either return the vegetables and bacon to the pan with the herbs, seasoning and wine and simmer for 30 minutes, or put all the ingredients in a casserole and cook in the centre of a moderately hot oven (200°C, 400°F, Gas Mark 6) for about 35–40 minutes.
4 Remove the chicken and keep warm on a dish. Reduce the sauce by boiling rapidly until just over 300 ml/½ pint remains then thicken by very gradually adding the beurre manié (butter creamed with the flour).
5 Reheat, stirring well. Pour over the chicken and serve with vegetables in season or French fried potatoes, and a green salad.

French fried potatoes: Peel and slice potatoes or cut into chip shapes and dry well. Heat deep oil or fat until a cube of day-old bread turns golden brown within 1 minute. Fry the potatoes until soft. Remove from the pan and reheat the oil or fat. Fry for a further 1–2 minutes until crisp and brown. Drain on absorbent paper.

Spanish-style chicken

you will need for 6–8 servings:

METRIC/IMPERIAL

giblets (optional)	2 tablespoons chopped parsley or mixed herbs
salt and pepper	
50–75 g/2–3 oz butter	1 large roasting chicken

for the sauce:

2 large onions	2 tablespoons oil
1–2 cloves garlic	chicken stock (optional)
3–4 large tomatoes	12 black olives
2 red peppers	12 green olives
2 green peppers	600 ml/1 pint chicken stock or water
225 g/8 oz long-grain rice	
pinch saffron powder	salt

1 If you would like to cook the sauce and the rice using chicken stock, simmer the giblets in water to cover and season well.
2 Blend the seasoning with the butter; mix half with the parsley or mixed herbs and put inside the bird, then spread the remaining butter over the breast of the bird and roast (see page 35).
3 Peel and slice the onions, peel and crush the garlic; skin and slice the tomatoes then cut the peppers into rings, discarding cores and seeds.
4 Heat the oil in a pan and fry the onions and garlic for 5 minutes, then add the rest of the vegetables and simmer until soft, adding a little chicken stock if the mixture seems too thick. Season well.
5 Put the rice with the saffron, stock or water and salt in a pan, bring to the boil and stir briskly; cover the pan and simmer steadily until soft.
6 Joint or carve the chicken neatly and add the olives to the sauce. Serve on a bed of rice topped with the sauce.

Note:
Saffron adds both colour and flavour to rice and is used in many countries for this purpose. Either buy

saffron powder and add a pinch to the liquid in which the rice is cooked, or first infuse a few strands of saffron for about 15 minutes, or longer, then strain if desired before cooking the rice. The sauce in this recipe freezes well; add the olives when reheating.

Variation:
Fried Spanish chicken: Season joints of young chicken and fry for a few minutes in hot oil or butter and oil until golden brown. Lift out of the pan then add a little more oil and proceed as stage 3. When the vegetables begin to soften return the chicken to the pan at stage 4 and continue cooking.

Chicken cacciatore

you will need for 6–8 servings:

METRIC/IMPERIAL	
4 sticks celery	1 teaspoon chopped fresh
2 onions or 12 spring	or ½ teaspoon dried
onions	marjoram
1 clove garlic	salt, cayenne and black
700 g/1½ lb cooked	pepper to taste
chicken and giblets	225 g/8 oz Patna, Italian
50 g/2 oz butter or	or long-grain rice
margarine	600 ml/1 pint chicken
2 tablespoons chopped	stock
parsley	50–100 g/2–4 oz Parmesan
1 (397-g/14-oz) can	cheese
tomatoes	
1 teaspoon chopped fresh	
or ½ teaspoon dried	
thyme	

1 Cut the celery into neat pieces, peel and chop the onion or spring onions and garlic.
2 Dice the cooked chicken and meat from the giblets.
3 Heat the butter or margarine in a pan and add the celery, onions, garlic and parsley.
4 Cook gently until nearly soft, stirring well, then add the chicken, tomatoes and juice from the can, herbs and seasoning and simmer in a covered pan for 20 minutes or until tender.
5 Meanwhile cook the rice in well seasoned chicken stock until tender.
6 Serve the chicken mixture on a bed of rice and sprinkle with grated Parmesan cheese.

Chicken Kiev

you will need for 4 servings:

METRIC/IMPERIAL	
2 small frying poussins	flour
or spring chickens	1 egg
100 g/4 oz butter	dried breadcrumbs
salt and pepper	

to fry:
oil or fat

1 Halve the chickens down the breastbone and carefully remove the flesh from all the bones but the drumstick, trying to keep the meat in one piece.
2 Flatten out each boned chicken half. Put a quarter of the butter on each portion at the end opposite the drumstick.
3 Roll the meat neatly from that end around the drumstick.
4 Skewer or tie and coat in seasoned flour.
5 Brush with beaten egg and roll in breadcrumbs.
6 Fry steadily in deep oil or fat for approximately 12–15 minutes (see page 24); drain on absorbent paper. Pierce the flesh just before serving to allow the butter to run out.

Variation:
Blend finely chopped parsley, fried chopped mushrooms or chopped cooked or canned red pepper with the butter.

Poulet sauté à la marengo

you will need for 6 servings:

METRIC/IMPERIAL	
1 young chicken	1 small cooked lobster (or
12 button mushrooms	canned lobster meat, or
12 small onions or shallots	fresh or canned prawns)
1 clove garlic	300 ml/½ pint brown
5 tablespoons oil	sauce (see page 42)
salt and pepper	300 ml/½ pint tomato
150 ml/¼ pint white wine	sauce (see page 43)
	6 eggs

to garnish:
chopped parsley   fried croûtons

1 Cut the chicken into small pieces, removing all bones if possible.
2 Wash the mushrooms, trim the base of the stalks but do not peel; peel the onions or shallots and leave whole; peel and crush the garlic.
3 Heat most of the oil in a large strong frying pan (with a lid). Fry the seasoned chicken with the onions or shallots and garlic for about 10 minutes until golden brown. Add mushrooms and continue cooking for 5 minutes then pour off any surplus oil.
4 Add the wine to the pan and heat gently for 5 minutes, covering the pan so the liquid does not evaporate.
5 Meanwhile remove fresh lobster meat from the shell and cut into neat pieces or drain the canned lobster. If using prawns instead, peel them or drain canned prawns. Stir the shellfish into the chicken mixture – do not heat for more than 1–2 minutes.
6 Spoon the chicken, lobster or prawns and vegetables on to a hot serving dish.
7 Add the brown and tomato sauces to any liquid remaining in the pan and heat together for a few minutes.
8 Heat any remaining oil and fry the eggs in a separate small frying pan.
9 Pour the sauce round, but not over, the chicken mixture. Top the dish with the fried eggs, chopped parsley, croûtons of fried bread and any lobster claws or extra whole prawns.

Note:
It is a good idea to fry the croûtons earlier in the day and just heat them in the oven while keeping the chicken mixture hot. For a more economical dish, omit the shellfish. This dish can be prepared in advance up to stage 5, but it is better not to pre-cook then reheat shellfish or it may become tough and leathery.

Variation:
Chicken with tarragon: A simpler but very delicious dish can be made by adding 1 tablespoon finely chopped fresh tarragon at stage 4. Omit the shellfish. sauces and eggs.

Chicken moussaka

you will need for 4–6 servings:
METRIC/IMPERIAL
for the sauce:

40 g/1½ oz butter	2 aubergines
40 g/1½ oz flour	2 potatoes
450 ml/¾ pint milk	2 onions
salt and pepper	3 tablespoons oil or
100–175 g/4–6 oz Cheddar	75 g/3 oz chicken fat
cheese	350–450 g/12 oz–1 lb
grated nutmeg	cooked chicken

1 First make the sauce with the butter, flour and milk (see page 41), season well then grate the cheese and add to the sauce with the grated nutmeg.
2 Slice the aubergines thinly, sprinkle lightly with salt and leave for 15–20 minutes, then rinse and pat dry. Peel and slice the potatoes and onions.
3 Fry the vegetables in the hot oil or fat until softened; season well.
4 Dice the chicken, mix with the vegetables and put half the mixture in a casserole; top with half the sauce then the rest of the chicken mixture.
5 Pour the remaining sauce over the chicken and vegetables, cover and cook in the centre of a moderate oven (180°C, 350°F, Gas Mark 4) for 45 minutes.

Variation:
Economy chicken moussaka: Omit the aubergines and use 4–5 potatoes. For a firmer dish use slightly less sauce.

Paella

you will need for 4–6 servings:
METRIC/IMPERIAL

2–4 young chicken joints	salt and pepper
1 onion	225 g/8 oz cooked or
1 clove garlic	frozen peas
2 medium tomatoes	1 small cooked lobster or
1 litre 150 ml/2 pints	canned lobster meat
chicken stock	8–10 large prawns
pinch saffron powder	6–8 mussels
2 tablespoons olive oil	1 fresh or canned red
100 g/4 oz Patna or long-	pepper
grain rice	

1 Cut the chicken into bite-size pieces, peel and chop the onion and garlic; skin and slice the tomatoes.
2 Blend the stock with the saffron powder.
3 Heat the oil in a very large frying pan and fry the chicken, onion and garlic until golden.
4 Pour in half the stock, bring to boiling point and simmer for 10 minutes; add the tomatoes, the rest of the stock, rice and seasoning. Stir briskly then lower the heat and simmer until rice is just tender.
5 If using frozen peas, put them in just before the rice is quite soft. If using cooked peas, add at stage 6.
6 Flake the lobster meat and add to the rice mixture with the cooked peas (if used), prawns, mussels and diced pepper.
7 Heat gently for a few minutes; by this time most of the liquid should have been absorbed, so stir gently with a fork during the final cooking period. Serve hot as soon as possible.

Variation:
A more economical paella can be made by omitting the lobster meat at stage 6. Add 50 g/2 oz sliced mushrooms with the tomatoes at stage 4.

Welsh leek and chicken pie

you will need for 6–8 servings:
METRIC/IMPERIAL

1 boiling fowl or roasting	shortcrust pastry made
chicken	with 225 g/8 oz flour
3 lambs' tongues	(see page 59)
salt and pepper	3–4 tablespoons double
3 sticks celery	cream
6 medium leeks	
1–2 tablespoons chopped	
parsley	

1 Put the fowl or chicken into a large pan and add the lambs' tongues, water to cover and seasoning to taste. Simmer steadily until tender (see page 17); the tongues should take about 1 hour to tenderise.
2 Chop the celery and add to the pan 40 minutes before the end of the cooking time.
3 Remove the chicken, tongues and celery from the liquid; boil rapidly in an open pan until reduced to barely 300 ml/½ pint.
4 Cut the chicken into neat pieces and skin and slice the tongues.
5 Cut the well-washed leeks into thin slices; arrange the meat and vegetables in a pie dish and sprinkle on the chopped parsley. Meanwhile make the pastry and allow the concentrated stock to cool slightly.
6 Roll out the pastry; cover the chicken with the stock, then with the pastry. Make a hole in the centre of the pastry and decorate with pastry leaves and a rose or tassel round the centre hole.
7 Bake the pie in the centre of a moderately hot oven (200°C, 400°F, Gas Mark 6) for 25 minutes until the pastry begins to brown well, then remove from the oven. Pour the cream through a small funnel into the hole in the top of the pastry.

8 Return the pie to the oven, lower the heat to moderate (180°C, 350°F, Gas Mark 4) and continue cooking for a further 20–25 minutes. Serve hot or cold.

Variation:
This is the traditional Welsh dish, but the filling may be varied by substituting chopped bacon for the lambs' tongues.

With a Chinese touch

The following recipes give an oriental touch to chicken. Remember that in Chinese cookery food should never be overcooked. It is cut into tiny pieces so that it cooks quickly and retains its texture.

Sweet and sour chicken

you will need for 4 servings:

METRIC/IMPERIAL	
450 g/1 lb raw young chicken	2 tablespoons brown malt vinegar
6–8 spring onions	½–1 tablespoon soy sauce
1 green pepper	1 tablespoon cornflour
2 tablespoons oil	1 (226-g/8-oz) can pineapple cubes
300 ml/½ pint chicken stock	salt and pepper
2 tablespoons brown sugar	

1 Cut the chicken into small pieces, skin then slice the onions and dice the pepper (discarding the core and seeds).
2 Heat the oil in a pan and fry the chicken and vegetables for 5 minutes.
3 Add the stock, sugar, vinegar and soy sauce and simmer for 15 minutes.
4 Blend the cornflour with the syrup from the can of pineapple, pour into the pan and stir until the sauce thickens. Tip in the pineapple cubes, add seasoning to taste and heat through for a few minutes. Serve with boiled rice.

Variation:
Fried chicken with sweet-sour sauce: Coat the diced chicken with a layer of well seasoned cornflour or flour. Fry the onions and pepper in just 1 tablespoon of oil at stage 2. Meanwhile fry the chicken in more oil until tender and crisp and brown on the outside.

Chicken with bamboo shoots

you will need for 4 servings:

METRIC/IMPERIAL	
1 large chicken breast	1 tablespoon cornflour
1–2 spring onions	2 tablespoons sherry
3 slices fresh ginger	2 tablespoons water
50 g/2 oz mushrooms	salt and pepper
1 (269-g/9½-oz) can bamboo shoots	3 tablespoons oil
	2 tablespoons soy sauce

1 Skin the chicken and cut into narrow strips; chop the onion and ginger and slice the mushrooms and drained bamboo shoots.
2 Blend the cornflour with the sherry, water, seasoning and chopped onion; add the chicken and ginger.
3 Put 1 tablespoon of the oil into a frying pan and cook the mushrooms in it for 2 minutes, stirring all the time; remove from the pan.
4 Put the remaining oil into the pan and when quite hot put in the chicken mixture; cook for 1 minute, stirring constantly.
5 Add the bamboo shoots and cook for 1 further minute.
6 Add the cooked mushrooms and soy sauce and heat thoroughly; serve at once with fried rice or fried noodles (see pages 53, 56).

Variation:
Add a well drained can of bean sprouts as well as, or instead of, the bamboo shoots. A few split almonds added at stage 5 give a pleasant crispness to the dish.

Chicken chop suey

you will need for 4 servings:

METRIC/IMPERIAL	
50 g/2 oz mushrooms	350 g/12 oz bean sprouts
300 ml/½ pint chicken stock	1 tablespoon fat or oil
	salt and pepper
2 large chicken legs	soy sauce
175 g/6 oz onions	pinch sugar
100 g/4 oz bamboo shoots	1 teaspoon cornflour

to serve:
fried noodles or fried rice

to garnish:
fried omelette

1 Chop the mushrooms finely and soak in the stock.
2 Cut the chicken from the bones in neat pieces to make about 225 g/8 oz meat.
3 Peel and slice the onions and slice the bamboo shoots.
4 Fry chicken pieces, onions, bean sprouts and bamboo shoots for a few minutes, taking care they do not discolour. Add the mushrooms and all but a tablespoon of the stock, together with seasoning, soy sauce and sugar, and cook gently for 25–35 minutes until the chicken is tender.
5 Blend the cornflour with remaining stock, add to the ingredients in the pan, bring to the boil and cook for 1 minute.
6 Pile on to a hot dish and serve with fried noodles or fried rice (see pages 53, 56). Garnish with fried omelette cut into strips (see below).

Fried omelette: Beat 2 eggs with salt and pepper. Heat 25 g/1 oz butter or oil in an omelette pan, pour in the eggs and allow to set. Cook the omelette in the usual way, allowing it to become quite firm. Turn out and cut into narrow strips.

Interesting Ideas for Small Quantities

In this section small amounts of chicken are used to make interesting and economical dishes. Many of the dishes are good for using up the tiny pieces of chicken left on a carcass; some are suitable for special occasions.

Freezing the dishes is quite satisfactory in most cases. As the chicken is already cooked, take care not to overcook when cooking the new dish.

Chicken à la king

This makes an ideal buffet party dish. Serve in a hot dish garnished with triangles or croûtons of crisp toast.

you will need for 4 servings:

METRIC/IMPERIAL

50 g/2 oz mushrooms	50 g/2 oz butter or
½–1 red or green pepper	margarine

for the sauce:

25 g/1 oz butter or chicken fat	salt and pepper
25 g/1 oz flour	1 egg
150 ml/¼ pint milk and 150 ml/¼ pint chicken stock or 300 ml/½ pint milk	2–3 tablespoons double cream
225–350 g/8–12 oz cooked chicken	

to serve:
4 large slices bread
butter

to garnish:
chopped parsley

1 Slice the mushrooms and pepper (discarding core and seeds).
2 Heat the butter or margarine in a pan, add the mushrooms and pepper and cook gently until soft.
3 Make a white sauce (see page 41); when thickened remove from the heat.
4 Blend the egg and cream together then whisk into the sauce; cook gently without boiling for 2–3 minutes.
5 Cut the chicken into neat pieces, add to the sauce with the cooked mushrooms and pepper and gently heat through for a few minutes, taking care the mixture does not boil.
6 Meanwhile toast the bread, spread with butter and top with the chicken mixture.
7 Garnish with chopped parsley and serve at once.

Note:
This dish freezes well, but it is better to omit stage 4 and add the egg and cream when reheating the dish. If you want to flavour the sauce with sherry (see below), add it when reheating.

Variations:
Sherry sauce: Add a little sherry to the sauce as well as, or instead of, the egg and cream at stage 4.
Sweet corn and lemon: Substitute cooked or canned sweet corn for the pepper. Use only 25 g/1 oz butter for frying the mushrooms. Flavour the sauce with a little lemon juice after adding the egg and cream.

Chicken au gratin

you will need for 4 servings:

METRIC/IMPERIAL

4 portions cooked chicken	75 g/3 oz hard cheese
300 ml/½ pint cheese sauce (see page 41)	3 tablespoons dried breadcrumbs
2 tablespoons double cream	25 g/1 oz butter

to garnish:
chopped parsley

1 Arrange the chicken in an ovenproof dish. Make the sauce, blend in the cream and pour over the chicken.
2 Grate the cheese, mix with the breadcrumbs and sprinkle over the sauce.
3 Dot with the butter.
4 Cook towards the top of a moderately hot oven (190°C, 375°F, Gas Mark 5) for 20–30 minutes. Serve garnished with chopped parsley.

Note:
The chicken portions can be heated in the sauce for a few minutes then put into a flameproof dish, topped with the grated cheese, crumbs and butter and browned under a hot grill for a few minutes.

Variations:
Chicken Florentine: Cook 450 g/1 lb spinach then sieve or chop finely and blend with 1–2 tablespoons cream if desired. Put into the ovenproof dish under the chicken.

Chicken soubise au gratin: Boil several large peeled whole onions in salted water, drain, chop neatly and blend with a little butter or cream. Put into the ovenproof dish under the chicken.

Chicken and eggs au gratin

you will need for 4 servings:

METRIC/IMPERIAL
4 eggs
175 g/6 oz cooked
  chicken

300 ml/½ pint cheese
  sauce (see page 41)

to garnish:
sprig of parsley   paprika

1 Hard-boil the eggs, shell and cool slightly.
2 Chop the chicken finely and blend with 1 tablespoon of the cheese sauce.
3 Halve the eggs and remove the yolks; mash the yolks and mix with the chicken.
4 Fill the halved whites with the chicken mixture and re-form the eggs. Put in an ovenproof dish, coat with the remaining cheese sauce and heat in the centre of a moderately hot oven (190°C, 375°F, Gas Mark 5).
5 Serve garnished with parsley and paprika.

Note:
Do not freeze this dish as the eggs would become tough and leathery.

Variation:
Stuffed eggs: Omit the cheese sauce and serve the eggs cold, topped with mayonnaise.

Chicken mornay

you will need for 4 servings:

METRIC/IMPERIAL
300 ml/½ pint cheese
  sauce (see page 41)
2 tablespoons cream

4 portions cooked
  chicken

to garnish:
2 slices bread
butter or chicken fat

sprigs of parsley

1 Make the sauce then blend in the cream.
2 Arrange the chicken in an ovenproof dish. Pour the sauce over the chicken and heat for 20–25 minutes in the centre of a moderate oven (180°C, 350°F, Gas Mark 4).
3 Cut the bread into triangles and fry in a little hot butter or chicken fat until brown on both sides.
4 Garnish with the crisp triangles and parsley sprigs.

Variations:
Chicken and vegetable pie: Blend about 225 g/8 oz cooked diced vegetables with the cooked chicken at stage 2. Top with grilled halved tomatoes before serving.

Chicken Milanaise: Substitute tomato sauce (see page 43) for the cheese sauce. Top with the crisp bread and serve with boiled rice or crispy fried noodles (see page 56).

Chicken in cheese and paprika sauce: Add 2 teaspoons paprika and 2 canned red peppers, drained and chopped, to the sauce at stage 1.

Chicken pan pie

you will need for 4–6 servings:

METRIC/IMPERIAL
1 onion
1 apple
2 sticks celery
350 g/12 oz cooked
  chicken
50 g/2 oz butter or
  margarine
1 teaspoon chopped
  marjoram (optional)

salt and pepper
450 ml/¾ pint chicken
  gravy (see page 38)
175 g/6 oz boiled rice
100 g/4 oz hard cheese
50 g/2 oz fine dried
  breadcrumbs

1 Peel and chop the onion and chop the unpeeled apple. Dice the celery and chicken.
2 Melt the butter or margarine in a large pan and fry the onion, apple and celery until lightly browned.
3 Add the chicken and marjoram if used, season well then pour the chicken gravy over the chicken mixture; add the rice. Mix thoroughly and turn into a casserole.
4 Cover and cook in the centre of a moderate oven (180°C, 350°F, Gas Mark 4) for 20 minutes.
5 Grate the cheese; sprinkle grated cheese and breadcrumbs on top of the chicken mixture and return uncovered to the oven; cook for a further 10 minutes.

Chicken quenelles

you will need for 4 servings:

METRIC/IMPERIAL
225 g/8 oz cooked chicken
25 g/1 oz butter or
  margarine
25 g/1 oz flour
150 ml/¼ pint milk or
  chicken stock
salt and pepper

1 egg
2 tablespoons soft
  breadcrumbs
2–4 long rashers streaky
  bacon
dried breadcrumbs

to fry:
fat or oil

to garnish:
chopped parsley   tomatoes

1 Put the cooked chicken through a mincer.
2 Heat the butter or margarine in a pan, stir in the flour and cook for several minutes.
3 Gradually add the milk or stock and bring to the boil, stirring constantly. Continue cooking until it is really thick then season.
4 Stir in the minced chicken, half the beaten egg and the breadcrumbs.
5 Form into 8 small sausage shapes.
6 Cut the rinds off the bacon rashers and cut into 8 pieces, each long enough to wrap round a chicken quenelle; secure with wooden cocktail sticks.
7 Dip the shapes in the remaining egg and coat thoroughly in dried breadcrumbs.
8 Heat the fat in a frying pan and fry the quenelles until crisp and brown, turning once or twice, or fry without turning in deep fat or oil.

9 Continue cooking slowly for a few minutes then drain on absorbent paper.
10 Garnish with parsley and fried or grilled tomatoes.

Variation:
Poached quenelles: Omit the bacon at stage 6 and the coating at stage 7. Pour 300 ml/½ pint milk or chicken stock into a frying pan and poach the quenelles for about 6 minutes. Lift out on to a hot dish. Make a white sauce (see page 41) with the milk or stock left in the pan plus extra milk as required. When thickened, whisk in the remaining egg.

Chicken ribbons

Coat strips of cooked or raw chicken in a little seasoned flour, then beaten egg and breadcrumbs, and fry until crisp and brown. If using up cooked chicken, just fry for about 2 minutes. For raw chicken fry as usual (see pages 23, 24). Always drain well on absorbent paper. Serve with tomato sauce (see page 43) or Tartare sauce (see page 80). These are very good for a cocktail party: put a cocktail stick through each piece of fried chicken and arrange on a dish with one or more sauces as dips.

Chicken shepherd's pie

you will need for 4 servings:
METRIC/IMPERIAL

I onion	salt and pepper
225 g/8 oz cooked chicken	450 g/I lb cooked potatoes
25–50 g/I–2 oz chicken fat	25 g/I oz butter
25 g/I oz flour	2 tablespoons milk
300 ml/½ pint stock	

1 Peel and chop or grate the onion; dice the chicken.
2 Melt the fat in a saucepan, add the onion and cook for 2–3 minutes; stir in the flour.
3 Gradually add the stock, stirring all the time. Bring to the boil and cook for 2–3 minutes.
4 Add the chicken and seasoning to the sauce. Pour into a 900-ml/1½-pint ovenproof dish.
5 Mash the potato with the butter and milk; season well. Spread over the chicken, mark with a fork and brown under the grill or in a moderately hot oven (190°C, 375°F, Gas Mark 5) for 15–20 minutes if the ingredients are hot; allow a longer period at a slightly lower temperature if the pie has been prepared ahead and become cold.

Creamed potato and chicken ring

This recipe is an ideal way of serving chicken to an invalid, for the dish both looks pleasant and is easy to eat. Chicken is an ideal food, easily digested and with a definite yet appetising taste.

you will need for I serving:
METRIC/IMPERIAL

100 g/4 oz cooked potatoes	I tomato
	salt and pepper
25 g/I oz butter	75 g/3 oz cooked chicken
150 ml/¼ pint milk	15 g/½ oz flour

1 Mash the potatoes with half the butter and 2 tablespoons of the milk; skin and slice the tomato and blend with the potato; season.
2 Form into a ring on a hot flameproof dish or plate. Put into the oven or under the grill to keep hot while the chicken mixture is prepared.
3 Dice or slice the chicken.
4 Heat the rest of the butter and stir in the flour. Cook gently for 2–3 minutes, then gradually add the remaining milk. Bring to the boil, stirring constantly.
5 Cook until thickened, add the chicken and season. Heat well then pour into the centre of the potato ring.

Chicken hash

you will need for 4 servings:
METRIC/IMPERIAL

350 g/12 oz cooked chicken	50 g/2 oz chicken or other fat
350 g/12 oz cooked potatoes	4–8 tablespoons chicken stock
3 onions	salt and pepper
to garnish:	
chopped parsley	

1 Cut the chicken into small pieces and mash with the potatoes.
2 Peel and slice the onions thinly and fry in hot fat in a large frying pan until tender.
3 Moisten the chicken and potato mixture with stock until it becomes the consistency of thick cream; season well.
4 Add the mixture to the onions in the pan, smoothing flat, and cook steadily until crisp and golden brown at the bottom and very hot.
5 Fold over like an omelette, tip on to a hot dish and garnish with chopped parsley.

Sour sweet chicken

you will need for 4 servings:
METRIC/IMPERIAL

4 large tomatoes	I tablespoon sugar
2–3 pieces celery	I teaspoon capers
300 ml/½ pint white wine or cider	350 g/12 oz cooked chicken
salt and pepper	

1 Skin and slice the tomatoes, chop the celery and put

with the wine or cider, seasoning, sugar and capers into a saucepan.

2 Simmer for about 30 minutes then add the chicken, cut into neat pieces, and continue simmering for 20 minutes.

Chicken toad-in-the-hole

you will need for 4 servings:
METRIC/IMPERIAL
for pancake batter:

100 g/4 oz plain flour	300 ml/½ pint milk or
pinch salt	milk and water
1 egg	25 g/1 oz fat
	4 sausages
175 g/6 oz cooked	2 rashers bacon
chicken	

1 Make a pancake batter (see page 88).
2 Heat the fat in an ovenproof dish in a hot to very hot oven (230–240°C, 450–475°F, Gas Mark 8–9) for a few minutes then put in the sausages and diced bacon and heat for another 5 minutes.
3 Cut the chicken into tiny pieces, add to the hot sausages then pour on the batter.
4 Cook for 15 minutes, then reduce the heat to moderately hot (200°C, 400°F, Gas Mark 6) until the batter is well risen and brown. Serve at once.

Chicken patties

The recipes in this section include chickenburgers, plus cutlets, rissoles etc. made from cooked chicken. For freezing, patties should be prepared then coated and frozen on open trays to prevent the coating sticking to the wrapping. When very hard, wrap and store. Use within 3 months. If desired, prepare, cook then freeze.

If serving chicken rissoles or similar dishes as a hot meal, make either a brown sauce (see page 42) with chicken stock, or one of the other sauces in the section (see pages 41–43).

Chickenburgers

you will need for 4–6 servings:
METRIC/IMPERIAL

1 onion	50 g/2 oz soft
350 g/12 oz raw chicken	breadcrumbs
25 g/1 oz chicken fat,	salt and pepper
butter or margarine	1 egg
to coat:	
salt and pepper	flour
to fry:	
oil or fat	

1 Peel and chop, mince or grate the onion and mince or chop the chicken.
2 Fry the onion until golden brown in the fat, butter or margarine.
3 Stir in the chicken, breadcrumbs and seasoning and bind with the beaten egg.
4 Divide into 4–6 equal portions and shape into round flat cakes. Coat well with seasoned flour.
5 To bake, put on a hot greased baking tray and bake towards the top of a hot oven (220°C, 425°F, Gas Mark 7) for 20–30 minutes, depending on the thickness of the cakes.
6 To fry, cook in hot oil or fat, allowing 6–8 minutes on each side. Reduce the heat after browning.
7 To grill, brush with hot oil or fat and cook for 6–8 minutes on each side.
8 Serve on hot toasted rolls or bread or as a main dish with vegetables.

Note:
These can be cooked from the frozen state, but do not cook and freeze.

Chicken croquettes

you will need for 4 servings:
METRIC/IMPERIAL
350 g/12 oz cooked
  chicken

for the sauce:	
25 g/1 oz chicken fat,	150 ml/¼ pint milk or
butter or margarine	chicken stock
25 g/1 oz flour	salt and pepper
to coat:	
flour	soft or dried
1 egg	breadcrumbs
to fry:	
oil or fat	

1 Mince or chop the chicken very finely.
2 Make a thick sauce with the fat, flour and milk or chicken stock (see page 41); season well.
3 Add the chicken and allow the mixture to cool slightly then form into croquette (finger) shapes.
4 Coat with a little flour, then beaten egg and breadcrumbs.
5 Fry in shallow or deep oil or fat until crisp and golden brown on each side then drain on absorbent paper; serve hot or cold.

Note:
The mixture can be formed into round flat cakes or cutlet shapes as well; either of these is easier to fry in shallow than deep oil or fat.

Variation:
Chicken and egg croquettes: Use 225 g/8 oz cooked chopped chicken and 2–3 chopped hard-boiled eggs.

Chicken darioles

you will need for 4 servings:

METRIC/IMPERIAL
2 small tomatoes	4 tablespoons milk
350 g/12 oz raw chicken	2 eggs or 2 egg yolks
4 tablespoons soft breadcrumbs	salt and pepper

1 Skin the tomatoes and pound or liquidise them.
2 Mince the chicken and add to the tomato purée with the rest of the ingredients.
3 Put into eight greased dariole tins, cover with greased greaseproof paper and steam for 30 minutes; serve with Allemande sauce (see page 41) or tomato purée.

Note:
This dish is not suitable for freezing.

Variation:
Chicken tomato darioles: Blend the tomato purée with *cooked* minced chicken, 25 g/1 oz melted butter or margarine, 40 g/1½ oz soft breadcrumbs, the milk, 2 eggs and seasoning. Steam for only 20 minutes.

Chicken cutlets

you will need for 6–8 servings:

METRIC/IMPERIAL
450 g/1 lb cooked chicken	200 ml/⅓ pint evaporated milk, single cream or milk
225 g/8 oz sausagemeat	
1 onion or shallot	
100 g/4 oz soft breadcrumbs	25 g/1 oz butter
	25 g/1 oz flour
	salt and pepper

to coat:
flour	soft or dried breadcrumbs
1 egg	

to fry:
50–75 g/2–3 oz fat

1 Mince the chicken and mix with the sausagemeat.
2 Peel and mince or chop the onion or shallot and put in a basin with the breadcrumbs and evaporated milk, cream or milk.
3 When the breadcrumbs are well moistened, strain off and reserve the liquid, pressing the bread with a fork to extract as much liquid as possible.
4 Melt the butter in a pan and stir in the flour, mixing well. Gradually add the strained milk or cream and cook until the sauce is smooth and the consistency of whipped cream. Add to the chicken mixture with the soaked breadcrumbs.
5 Season to taste and divide the mixture into 6–8 portions or 12–16 smaller pieces. Mould into cutlet shapes with damp hands, dust lightly with flour then coat with beaten egg and breadcrumbs.
6 Fry slowly in hot fat, turning once or twice, until the cutlets are crisp and brown; drain on absorbent paper.

Note:
It is essential to cook the mixture steadily rather than quickly to be sure the sausagemeat is cooked.

Chicken and ham rissoles

In this recipe gelatine has been included, making possible a moist texture. When cold the mixture sets sufficiently for handling, and when fried it becomes soft again.

you will need for 4 servings:

METRIC/IMPERIAL
275–350 g/10–12 oz cooked chicken	1 teaspoon gelatine
	4 tablespoons milk or single cream
100 g/4 oz cooked ham or boiled bacon	1 tablespoon chopped parsley
1 onion	
50 g/2 oz butter, margarine or chicken fat	1 teaspoon chopped lemon thyme
	40 g/1½ oz soft breadcrumbs
25 g/1 oz flour	salt and pepper
175 ml/6 fl oz chicken stock	

to coat:
salt and pepper	50 g/2 oz soft breadcrumbs
flour	
1 egg	

to fry:
fat or oil

1 Mince or finely chop nearly all the chicken and ham or boiled bacon. Leave a few larger pieces to give an interesting combination of textures.
2 Peel and chop the onion, then heat the butter or other fat and fry the onion until soft.
3 Stir in the flour, then 150 ml/¼ pint of the stock; bring to the boil and cook until thickened.
4 Meanwhile soften the gelatine in the remaining stock and add to the hot sauce; stir until dissolved.
5 Pour in the milk or cream, add the herbs, all the chicken and ham or bacon and the breadcrumbs; season well. Allow the mixture to cool and stiffen slightly, then form into small round cakes.
6 Coat in seasoned flour, then beaten egg and breadcrumbs; fry in shallow fat or oil until crisp and golden brown. Serve hot.

Variations:
Chicken and ham balls: Form the mixture into small balls instead of cakes. Deep fry. These are delicious if put on to cocktail sticks and served as a snack.

Surprise chicken balls: Mould the chicken ball mixture round stuffed green olives then coat and fry.

Chicken and potato cutlets

you will need for 4 servings:

METRIC/IMPERIAL
225 g/8 oz cooked chicken
6–8 stoned olives or small
  gherkins

225 g/8 oz mashed potato
salt and pepper
I egg

to coat:
50 g/2 oz soft
  breadcrumbs

to fry:
50 g/2 oz fat

to garnish:
watercress

1 Chop or mince the chicken finely; chop the olives or gherkins.
2 Blend with the mashed potato, seasoning and egg.
3 Form into cutlet shapes and coat with the crumbs; the mixture will be soft so beaten egg is not needed.
4 Heat the fat in a pan, fry the cutlets for about 2 minutes on each side then lower the heat and cook slowly for about 5 minutes; drain on absorbent paper.
5 Garnish with watercress and serve hot.

Chicken rice cutlets

you will need for 4 servings:

METRIC/IMPERIAL
225 g/8 oz cooked chicken
50 g/2 oz cooked Patna
  or long-grain rice
150 ml/$\frac{1}{4}$ pint panada
  consistency white sauce
  (see page 41)

6–8 stoned olives or small
  gherkins
salt and pepper
I egg

to coat:
50 g/2 oz soft
  breadcrumbs

to fry:
50 g/2 oz fat

to garnish:
watercress

1 Chop or mince the chicken finely and blend with the rice, thick white sauce, chopped olives or gherkins, seasoning and egg.
2 Form into cutlet shapes and coat with the crumbs; the mixture will be soft so beaten egg is not needed.
3 Fry steadily on each side in hot fat; lower the heat and cook gently for a further 8 minutes.
4 Drain on absorbent paper and serve hot, garnished with watercress.

Salads and Moulds

Chicken is probably one of the most popular foods for serving cold with a salad. Following a few guidelines will give best results. Make sure the chicken is freshly jointed or sliced, as the flesh dries very quickly if exposed to the air for any length of time. If you have to cut the chicken early then cover with foil, a polythene bag, damp kitchen paper or damp napkins.

Be adventurous in the selection of ingredients you put with the chicken. While it blends with most salad ingredients, it is particularly delicious with fruit, sweet corn and cheese. A good dressing is often the secret of a first-class salad; it is worth taking a little time to be sure of best results.

Classic mayonnaise

you will need for 4 servings:

METRIC/IMPERIAL

1 egg yolk	½–1 tablespoon white
pinch salt	wine vinegar or lemon
pepper	juice
dry mustard	½ tablespoon hot water
up to 150 ml/¼ pint olive oil	

1 Put the egg yolk, salt, pepper and mustard into a basin.
2 Very gradually beat in the oil, drop by drop, stirring all the time until the mixture thickens (adding too much at once will make the mixture curdle).
3 Gradually beat in the vinegar or lemon juice then the hot water (the water is not essential but gives a light creamy texture).

Variations:

Liquidiser mayonnaise: You may need to use 2 egg yolks and double quantities to cover the blades. A lighter-textured mayonnaise can be made by using whole eggs. Put the egg yolk or eggs, seasonings and vinegar or lemon juice into the liquidiser goblet, switch on for a few seconds then add the oil steadily through the top with the motor running, either by removing the cap from the lid or making a foil funnel or lid with a hole in the centre to cover the top of the goblet. Add the hot water at the end.

Herb mayonnaise: Add finely chopped parsley, chives, sage and thyme to the mayonnaise.

Tarragon mayonnaise: Add a little chopped fresh tarragon and a few drops of tarragon vinegar to the mayonnaise.

Tartare sauce (cold): Add a little chopped parsley, gherkins and capers to the mayonnaise.

Note:

Other flavourings such as extra lemon juice and finely grated lemon rind, horseradish, curry powder or tomato purée can be added to the mayonnaise. Do not try to freeze mayonnaise as it will probably separate; store in the refrigerator.

French dressing

you will need for 4 servings:

METRIC/IMPERIAL

4–6 tablespoons salad oil	2–3 tablespoons white or
made mustard	red wine vinegar, malt
pinch sugar	vinegar or lemon juice
salt and pepper	

1 Blend the oil with a little mustard, sugar and seasoning then gradually add the vinegar or lemon juice.
2 Alternatively, put all the ingredients into a screw top jar and shake hard or liquidise them together.

Variation:

Add chopped herbs and/or crushed garlic.

Salad cream

you will need for 4 servings:

METRIC/IMPERIAL

25 g/1 oz flour	25 g/1 oz butter,
1 teaspoon sugar	margarine or 1
½ teaspoon salt	tablespoon oil
pinch pepper	1 egg
pinch dry mustard	2 tablespoons white wine
300 ml/½ pint milk	vinegar or lemon juice

1 Mix the flour, sugar, seasoning and mustard together with a little of the cold milk.
2 Bring the remaining milk to the boil and pour over the dry ingredients, stirring thoroughly.
3 Put the mixture back into the same saucepan, adding the butter, margarine or oil and beaten egg.
4 Cook very slowly until the sauce coats the back of a wooden spoon.
5 Remove from the heat and whisk in the vinegar or lemon juice.
6 Pour at once into a screw top jar.

Note:

This salad cream will keep for several days if stored in a refrigerator. It freezes quite well and can be kept for 3–4 weeks.

Chicken cream slaw

you will need for 4 servings:

METRIC/IMPERIAL

2 teaspoons made mustard
150 ml/¼ pint soured
  cream or double cream
  plus 1 tablespoon lemon
  juice
½ teaspoon paprika
¼–½ teaspoon salt

pinch pepper
2 teaspoons lemon juice
225 g/8 oz white cabbage
1 medium green pepper
  (optional)
225–350 g/8–12 oz
  cooked chicken

1 Put the mustard in a small bowl and gradually stir in the soured cream, paprika, salt, pepper and lemon juice.
2 Shred the cabbage and pepper if used (discarding the core and seeds); cut the chicken into matchsticks then blend all the ingredients together.

Variation:
Omit the chicken and serve the salad with hot or cold chicken dishes.

Chicken Caesar salad

you will need for 4–6 servings:

METRIC/IMPERIAL

2–3 eggs
2–3 slices bread
50 g/2 oz butter
1 clove garlic
1 lettuce
450 g/1 lb cooked chicken

2–3 tomatoes
mayonnaise (see page 80)
50 g/2 oz hard cheese,
  grated
1 (56-g/2-oz) can anchovy
  fillets

1 Hard-boil the eggs; discard crusts and cut the bread into 1-cm/½-inch dice.
2 Heat the butter and fry the bread until crisp and brown. Drain on absorbent paper.
3 Peel and halve the garlic clove and rub round the salad bowl then shred the washed and dried lettuce into the bowl.
4 Cut the chicken into small pieces and slice the tomatoes and the shelled hard-boiled eggs.
5 Spoon the chicken, tomatoes and eggs over the lettuce then top with mayonnaise, grated cheese, croûtons of fried bread and a lattice of well drained anchovy fillets. Serve as soon as possible while the bread is crisp.

Chicken stuffed tomatoes

you will need for 4 servings:

METRIC/IMPERIAL

4 large tomatoes
1 hard-boiled egg

100–175 g/4–6 oz cooked
  chicken
salt and pepper

to serve:
mayonnaise (see page 80)
½ cucumber

lettuce leaves

1 Cut the tops off the tomatoes, scoop out then chop the centre pulp.
2 Shell and chop the egg and chop the chicken; blend with the tomato pulp and season lightly.
3 Pile the mixture back into the tomato cases.
4 Top with mayonnaise and a twist of cucumber; serve on a bed of lettuce and cucumber.

Salad Isabella

you will need for 4 servings:

METRIC/IMPERIAL

450 g/1 lb cooked chicken
150 ml/¼ pint mayonnaise
  (see page 80)
1 teaspoon paprika

75 g/3 oz boiled Patna or
  long-grain rice
salt and pepper to taste

to serve:
lettuce leaves

to garnish:
cooked or canned
  asparagus tips
  (optional)

1 Dice or slice the chicken into small neat pieces.
2 Blend with the mayonnaise, paprika and cooked rice, adding extra seasoning to taste.
3 Pile on to a bed of lettuce and garnish with a few asparagus tips if liked.

Spring chicken salad

you will need for 4–6 servings:

METRIC/IMPERIAL

2 eggs
350 g/12 oz cooked
  chicken
1 small celery heart
2–3 canned pineapple
  rings
2 tablespoons chopped
  almonds

2 tablespoon salad oil
2 tablespoons lemon juice
salt and pepper
15 g/½ oz gelatine
450 ml/¾ pint chicken
  stock or water

to garnish:
chopped parsley

1 Hard-boil then shell the eggs and chop the whites.
2 Cut the chicken into neat pieces, dice the celery and pineapple and mix with the almonds and egg whites.
3 Blend the oil, lemon juice and seasoning, then add the chicken mixture and leave for 30 minutes.
4 Dissolve the gelatine in the hot stock or water (see page 14).
5 Cool the gelatine liquid but do not allow it to set; blend with the chicken mixture.
6 Brush a 1-litre/1¾-pint mould or 4–6 individual moulds with a very little oil and spoon in the chicken mixture; leave until firm.
7 Turn out and sieve the egg yolks over the top; garnish with a layer of chopped parsley.

Note:

Do not use fresh pineapple or the mould will not set.

Variation:

Omit 1 tablespoon of the lemon juice and the gelatine and substitute lemon-flavoured jelly.

Easy chicken salads

The following salads serve 4–6 unless otherwise stated and are based on 225–350 g/8–12 oz cooked chicken.

Apple salad: Core 4–6 dessert apples and cut into rings. Arrange on a bed of green salad. Sprinkle with French dressing (see page 80). Dice the chicken and blend with mayonnaise (see page 80), chopped nuts and chopped dates. Pile on to the apple rings and top with chopped nuts.

Avocado salad: Peel then halve and slice 2 avocados, removing the stones. Toss in mayonnaise flavoured with a little extra lemon juice (see page 80). Mix with the sliced chicken and de-seeded grapes; spoon on to a bed of lettuce.

Celery salad: Blend the diced chicken with 225 g/8 oz chopped celery and 1 chopped and cored dessert apple. Bind with 150 ml/¼ pint mayonnaise (see page 80). Pile on to a bed of lettuce and garnish with chopped parsley and a few chopped blanched almonds.

Cheese log: Grate 225 g/8 oz Cheddar cheese and cut up 225 g/8 oz chicken finely. Mix with the cheese, 4–6 tablespoons peeled diced cucumber, 1–2 chopped red peppers (discarding core and seeds), 2 skinned chopped tomatoes, 2 teaspoons capers and enough mayonnaise (see page 80) to bind. Form into a log shape; wrap in foil then chill overnight or for several hours in the refrigerator. Lift on to a dish, garnish with green salad and cut into neat slices. Add 2–3 chopped hard-boiled eggs to the cheese mixture if liked.

Chef's salad: Cut the cooked chicken, 100–175 g/4–6 oz cooked ham, 100–175 g/4–6 oz cooked tongue and 100–175 g/4–6 oz Gruyère cheese into matchsticks. Toss in a mixture of French dressing and mayonnaise (see page 80), arrange on a bed of lettuce and garnish with chopped nuts. Serves up to 8.

Chicken and pepper salad: Cut a slice from the stalk ends of two green peppers and scoop out the core and centre seeds. Mix the finely chopped chicken with 100 g/4 oz grated cheese or cream cheese, 4 tablespoons mayonnaise (see page 80), 1 chopped red pepper, 2 chopped gherkins, 2 large skinned chopped tomatoes and the finely chopped slices of green pepper. Season and pack into the centre cavities of the green peppers. Using a sharp knife, cut the peppers horizontally into slices and arrange the rings on a bed of lettuce.

Cottage cheese salad: Mix equal quantities of cottage cheese and diced chicken. Spoon on to a bed of lettuce and garnish with grapes, pineapple, chopped parsley or chives.

Curried salad: Mix 1–2 teaspoons curry paste with 150 ml/¼ pint mayonnaise (see page 80). Blend with the diced chicken and add 1–2 tablespoons desiccated coconut, 1–2 tablespoons sultanas and 100 g/4 oz cooked rice. Serve on a bed of well seasoned sliced tomatoes and cucumber.

Ham cornets: Dice the chicken neatly and blend with 1 tablespoon chopped parsley, 100–175 g/4–6 oz diced cooked potatoes and 1–2 teaspoons capers. Twist 6 thin slices of ham into cornet shapes and fill with the mixture. Secure with cocktail sticks if necessary.

Hollandaise salad: Cut the chicken into neat joints or slices. Arrange on a bed of lettuce with quartered or halved hard-boiled eggs placed round. Coat with Hollandaise sauce (see page 30) and garnish with chopped parsley and/or paprika.

Macaroni salad: Combine the diced chicken with 175 g/6 oz cooked and cooled elbow or shell macaroni, 1 small diced cucumber, ½ tablespoon grated onion or chopped spring onion, 1 teaspoon finely chopped parsley, 150 ml/¼ pint mayonnaise (see page 80) and seasoning to taste. Toss until well blended.

Mushroom salad: Heat 25 g/1 oz butter in a saucepan and fry 100 g/4 oz sliced mushrooms until just tender. Put in a basin and mix with the sliced or diced chicken, 100 g/4 oz chopped celery, a few sliced olives (optional) and seasoning. Pile on to a bed of lettuce and garnish with more sliced olives. Raw sliced button mushrooms can be substituted for the fried ones.

Orange salad: Cut the chicken into small pieces. Peel 2–3 fresh oranges and remove the pulp in neat pieces, discarding pith and skin. Mix with the chicken then toss in French dressing (see page 80). Pile on to a bed of lettuce and garnish with watercress.

Pyramid salad: Mix the minced or finely chopped chicken with 1 tablespoon Worcestershire sauce, 1 tablespoon chopped parsley, 2 small sliced tomatoes, 50 g/2 oz sliced cucumber, 1 teaspoon oil and 1 tablespoon finely chopped chutney or mustard pickle. Season well, form into a pyramid on a bed of lettuce and garnish with rings of sliced beetroot and tomatoes.

Slimmers' salads

Dice 225–350 g/8–12 oz chicken and blend with any of the following suggestions. Use seasoned low-calorie yogurt and chopped herbs as a dressing.

Pineapple and chicken salad: Blend fresh diced pineapple with the chicken just before serving.

Grapefruit cups: Halve 2–3 grapefruit, remove the pulp and blend with the diced chicken and natural yogurt. Put shredded lettuce inside the grapefruit shells and top with the chicken and grapefruit mixture.

Hot and cold moulds

Chicken is excellent in moulds as it blends with most flavours and the other ingredients give a moist texture to lean chicken meat.

To prepare jellied moulds, either rinse the mould with cold water and shake out the surplus liquid, but do not dry, or brush the inside with a little salad or olive oil. To turn out either dip into hot water for a few seconds or wrap a hot tea towel round the outside for a few seconds then invert on to the serving dish. If this dish is moistened it will be easier to slide the mould into the centre.

For baked galantines etc., grease the tin or mould well and coat if suggested in the recipe. The purpose of standing the container in a tin of cold water in the oven is to keep the mixture moist.

Do not store frozen jellied moulds for more than a few days as they tend to become too stiff. Baked galantines etc. can be kept frozen for several weeks.

Chicken and tomato ring

you will need for 4–6 servings:

METRIC/IMPERIAL
450 g/1 lb tomatoes	50 g/2 oz hard cheese
bunch fresh chives	225 g/8 oz cooked chicken
salt and pepper	2 tablespoons double
600 ml/1 pint chicken	cream
stock	1 tablespoon mayonnaise
15 g/½ oz gelatine	1 tablespoon chopped
2 tablespoons water	parsley

to garnish:
watercress

1 Skin and chop the tomatoes and snip half the chives; simmer in well seasoned stock until it makes 600 ml/1 pint pulp then sieve or liquidise.
2 Soften the gelatine in the cold water, add to the hot tomato mixture and stir until dissolved.
3 Pour into an oiled ring mould and leave to set.
4 Grate the cheese, chop the chicken and snip the

remaining chives. Blend the cheese, chicken and chives with the cream, mayonnaise, parsley and more seasoning to taste.
5 Turn the tomato ring from the mould on to a serving dish and fill the centre with the cheese and chicken mixture; garnish with watercress.

Variation:
Chicken and cucumber ring: Omit the tomatoes and substitute a peeled diced cucumber; simmer in the stock at stage 1. Add diced green and red pepper (discarding the core and seeds) to the chicken mixture at stage 4.

Chicken and veal ring

you will need for 6–8 servings:

METRIC/IMPERIAL
450 g/1 lb stewing veal	salt and pepper
1 onion	2 teaspoons gelatine
1–2 carrots	1 tablespoon white wine
6 peppercorns	vinegar
2 bay leaves	450 g/1 lb cooked chicken
900 ml/1½ pints water	

for filling:
Russian salad

to serve:
sliced beetroot	lettuce leaves

1 Dice the veal, peel and chop the vegetables and put into a saucepan with the peppercorns and bay leaves.
2 Add the water, season well then cover with a tightly fitting lid and simmer for 1–1¼ hours.
3 Lift out the meat and allow to cool. Boil the stock in an open pan until there is just *under* 300 ml/½ pint. Dissolve the gelatine in the stock and add the vinegar and extra seasoning if desired.
4 Cut the chicken into neat pieces and arrange in an oiled ring mould with the diced veal.
5 Strain the gelatine liquid over the meat and allow to set. Turn out and fill the centre with Russian salad (see below). Serve with beetroot and lettuce.

Russian salad: Blend diced cooked root vegetables, cooked peas and beans with mayonnaise or salad cream (see page 80) and chopped parsley.

Tomato rascals

you will need for 4–8 servings:

METRIC/IMPERIAL
25 g/1 oz powdered	chives or spring onions
gelatine	225 g/8 oz cooked chicken
600 ml/1 pint chicken	2 tablespoons chopped
stock	parsley
8 large tomatoes	salt and pepper

to serve:
lettuce leaves

1 Dissolve the gelatine in the stock (see page 14).

2 Cut the tomatoes in half, scoop out the pulp and sieve into the stock.
3 Chop a few chives or onions and the chicken. Add with the chopped parsley and seasoning to taste to the tomato and gelatine mixture.
4 When the mixture is cold and just beginning to set, spoon into the tomato cases.
5 When quite firm lift on to a bed of lettuce.

Chicken galantine (1)

you will need for 4–6 servings:

METRIC/IMPERIAL

25 g/1 oz chicken fat or butter	225 g/8 oz sausagemeat
25 g/1 oz flour	50 g/2 oz soft breadcrumbs
150 ml/¼ pint chicken stock	1 egg
350 g/12 oz raw chicken	salt and pepper

1 Heat the chicken fat or butter in a pan. Stir in the flour and cook for several minutes.
2 Add the stock, bring to the boil and cook gently until thick.
3 Mince or dice the chicken very finely and blend with the sauce and the rest of the ingredients.
4 Press into a greased 1-kg/2-lb tin or mould, cover with greased foil and steam over boiling water for 1½ hours or stand in a tin of water and bake in the centre of a moderate oven (160°C, 325°F, Gas Mark 3) for 1¼ hours. Leave to cool.
5 Place a light weight on top of the galantine as it cools in the tin or mould. When set, it can be coated with aspic jelly or chaudfroid sauce (see pages 19, 40) and garnished as suggested in those recipes.

Note:
The mixture can also be formed into a roll then wrapped in greased greaseproof paper and steamed as stage 4.

Variations:
Chicken galantine (2): Bone a whole roasting chicken (see page 7). Simmer the bones for stock before cooking the galantine. Blend 450 g/1 lb sausagemeat with 100–175 g/4–6 oz chopped bacon, 50 g/2 oz soft breadcrumbs, 2 eggs, 1 tablespoon chopped parsley and the grated rind and juice of 1 lemon and season well. Spread over the chicken, roll up firmly and tie or skewer. Put into the chicken stock and simmer very gently until tender, approximately 2 hours. Allow to cool then coat the galantine with aspic jelly or chaudfroid sauce and garnish.

Chicken loaf: Use the same ingredients as for chicken galantine (2) (above), but reduce the amount of sausagemeat to 225 g/8 oz and add 1 onion. Peel and chop the onion and fry in 25 g/1 oz fat. Remove the chicken meat from the bones, mince it then blend with the sausagemeat, minced or chopped bacon, breadcrumbs, eggs, parsley, lemon juice and rind, fried onion and 4 tablespoons chicken stock. Prepare as for chicken galantine (1), stage 4 (you will need a 1·5-kg/3-lb tin or mould), but steam for nearly 2 hours or bake for 1½ hours. Serve hot or cold.

Crispy chicken loaf: Prepare as for chicken loaf (above), but grease the tin and coat with crushed potato crisps or dried breadcrumbs. Bake without standing in a tin of water. When cooked but still hot, top with crushed potato crisps.

Jellied chicken

you will need for 4 servings:

METRIC/IMPERIAL

600 ml/1 pint chicken stock	salt and pepper
1 onion	2 eggs
1 stick celery	450 g/1 lb cooked chicken
1–2 bay leaves	15 g/½ oz gelatine

to serve:
lettuce leaves

to garnish:

tomato slices	cucumber slices

1 If the stock is not well flavoured, use about 750 ml/1¼ pints stock, put in the peeled whole onion, chopped celery and bay leaves with a little additional seasoning if needed. Simmer gently in a covered pan for 30 minutes until reduced to 600 ml/1 pint.
2 Hard-boil, then shell and slice the eggs and cut the chicken into neat pieces.
3 Remove the vegetables from the stock, dissolve the gelatine in the stock (see page 14) and allow it to get cold, but not to set.
4 Pour the stock over the chicken and hard-boiled eggs and transfer to a rinsed mould.
5 When set, turn out on to a bed of lettuce and garnish with sliced tomatoes and cucumber.

Note:
You can dissolve aspic jelly in 600 ml/1 pint chicken stock or water instead of using gelatine.

Variations:
Chicken and vegetable mould: Add cooked peas, asparagus tips, diced carrots and other vegetables at stage 4. If using juicy vegetables such as diced cucumber, use just under 600 ml/1 pint liquid.

Chaudfroid mould: Use only 300 ml/½ pint chicken stock. Add 300 ml/½ pint *thin* mayonnaise (see page 80) plus 1 tablespoon sherry at stage 3. If using thick mayonnaise, dilute it with a little top of the milk to make a pouring consistency.

Mimosa chicken mould

you will need for 4 servings:

METRIC/IMPERIAL
225–350 g/8–12 oz cooked chicken
25 g/1 oz flour
25 g/1 oz butter
50 g/2 oz soft breadcrumbs
1 egg

150 ml/¼ pint single cream or evaporated milk
salt and pepper
Hollandaise sauce (see page 30)
1 hard-boiled egg yolk

to garnish:
lemon or tomato slices or asparagus tips

1 Dice or mince the chicken and blend with the flour, melted butter, breadcrumbs, beaten egg, cream or milk and seasoning.
2 Pour into a greased 900-ml/1½-pint basin or mould, cover with greased greaseproof paper or foil and steam until firm, about 1 hour.
3 Coat with the Hollandaise sauce and sprinkle sieved hard-boiled egg yolk over the top; garnish with lemon or tomato slices or asparagus tips and serve hot.

Mushroom-stuffed chicken loaf

you will need for 6–8 servings:

METRIC/IMPERIAL
for the stuffing:
1 onion
225 g/8 oz mushrooms
50 g/2 oz butter or margarine
1 teaspoon lemon juice
175 g/6 oz soft breadcrumbs

salt and pepper
½ teaspoon chopped fresh or ¼ teaspoon dried thyme
2 tablespoons chopped parsley

700 g/1½ lb raw chicken
2 eggs
4 tablespoons milk

2 tablespoons tomato ketchup
1 teaspoon dry mustard

1 Peel and chop the onion finely; slice all but 6 of the mushrooms.
2 Heat the butter or margarine and fry the onion and sliced mushrooms for 3–4 minutes; add the lemon juice, 100 g/4 oz of the breadcrumbs, the seasoning and herbs.
3 Mince or chop the raw chicken and mix with the beaten eggs, more seasoning, milk, ketchup, dry mustard and remaining breadcrumbs.
4 Pack half the chicken mixture into a greased 1-kg/2-lb loaf tin and spread the stuffing over.
5 Top with the remaining chicken mixture and press down firmly.
6 Place the 6 whole mushrooms on top and cover with greased foil. Stand the loaf tin in a tin of cold water and bake in the centre of a moderate oven (180°C, 350°F, Gas Mark 4) for 1¼ hours. Serve hot.

Variations:
Chicken and ham loaf: Use 350 g/12 oz raw chicken and 350 g/12 oz cooked boiled bacon or ham at stage 3.

Chicken and tongue loaf: Use 350 g/12 oz raw chicken and 350 g/12 oz cooked tongue at stage 3.

Sweet and sour chicken loaf

you will need for 4 servings:

METRIC/IMPERIAL
1 (397-g/14-oz) can tomatoes
700 g/1½ lb cooked chicken
1 onion
50 g/2 oz salted biscuits or potato crisps

1 tablespoon brown sugar
2 tablespoons white wine vinegar
1 teaspoon made mustard
1 egg
1½ teaspoons salt
¼ teaspoon pepper

1 Sieve or liquidise the tomatoes to make a smooth purée, adding the juice from the can.
2 Mince the chicken and peeled onion and crush the biscuits or crisps.
3 Mix the tomato purée in a saucepan with the brown sugar, vinegar and mustard. Stir over a medium heat until the sugar dissolves.
4 Combine the egg, minced chicken and onion, crushed salted biscuits or crisps, salt and pepper with 4 tablespoons of the tomato mixture.
5 Mix thoroughly and shape into a loaf; place on a baking tray. Pour the remaining tomato mixture over the loaf.
6 Bake in the centre of a moderate oven (160°C, 325°F, Gas Mark 3) for 1 hour, basting frequently with the sauce.
7 Lift the loaf on to a warm dish and serve the sauce separately or poured over the loaf.

Sausage and chicken ring

you will need for 4 servings:

METRIC/IMPERIAL
350 g/12 oz raw chicken
1 onion
350 g/12 oz sausagemeat
1 tablespoon tomato ketchup
¼ teaspoon celery salt
salt and pepper

½ teaspoon chopped basil or sage
1 small slice bread
1 egg
1 (99-g/3½-oz) packet sage and onion stuffing mix or dried breadcrumbs

1 Chop the chicken fairly finely and peel and grate the onion.
2 Mix with the sausagemeat, ketchup, celery salt, seasoning and basil or sage.
3 Cut off the crusts and soak the slice of bread in the

beaten egg then blend into the rest of the mixture with a fork.

4 Grease a 900-ml/1½-pint ring mould and dust with a little dry stuffing mix or breadcrumbs.

5 Press the sausage and chicken mixture into the ring and bake in the centre of a moderately hot oven (200°C, 400°F, Gas Mark 6) for 45 minutes; turn out and serve cold with salad.

Note:
Use the meat from 2 uncooked chicken legs.

Tomato chicken mould

you will need for 6 servings:

METRIC/IMPERIAL

1 small raw chicken	2 eggs
2–3 rashers bacon	salt and pepper
tomato sauce (see page 43)	
50 g/2 oz soft breadcrumbs	

1 Cut the meat from the chicken; use the bones for stock.

2 Mince the chicken meat with the derinded bacon rashers and mix with the tomato sauce, breadcrumbs, eggs and seasoning.

3 Spoon into a greased 1·5-litre/2½-pint basin and cover with greased foil. Steam steadily for 1¾ hours. Turn out and serve hot with gravy made from chicken stock.

Variations:

Creamy mould: Substitute white sauce (see page 41) for tomato sauce; add 1 tablespoon chopped parsley.

Chicken and tongue mould: Use white sauce as for creamy mould (above), but mince the dark meat of the chicken and dice the breast meat with 175 g/6 oz cooked tongue.

Light as a feather

This chapter covers omelettes, chicken creams and mousses, pancakes, soufflés, sandwiches and toasted snacks. These dishes are ideal for light family or party meals and equally suitable for invalids.

The combination of chicken and a light omelette mixture provides an easily digested and appetising light meal. Heat the chicken mixture before you make the omelette so the two can be served together without delay. Omelettes cannot be frozen, but frozen eggs can be used.

Delicate creams and mousses do not freeze well and are better freshly made. If you do freeze them, use within 2 weeks.

Pancake batter can be frozen before or after cooking. Use uncooked batter within 1 month. Cooked pancakes can be stored for up to 3 months: cook the pancakes, separate with squares of oiled greaseproof paper and wrap the pile in foil; you can then peel off the required number of pancakes for reheating.

Chicken omelette

you will need for each person:

METRIC/IMPERIAL
175–225 g/6–8 oz cooked chicken
40 g/1½ oz butter

2 eggs
½–1 tablespoon water
salt and pepper

to garnish:
sprigs of parsley

1 Dice the chicken neatly. Heat nearly 25 g/1 oz butter in a pan and heat the chicken for 2–3 minutes.
2 Meanwhile beat the eggs in a basin with the water and seasoning; tip in the hot chicken.
3 Heat the rest of the butter in an omelette pan, pour in the chicken and egg mixture and allow to set in a thin skin at the bottom of the pan.
4 Tilt the omelette pan and, using a palette knife or fish slice, loosen the setting omelette round the sides so the liquid egg mixture can run underneath.
5 Fold or roll, tip on to a hot dish or plate and serve at once, garnished with parsley.

Variations:
Soufflé omelette: Heat the diced chicken in a little cream or white or other sauce (see pages 41, 42) at stage 1. Separate the eggs and beat only the yolks with the water and seasoning at stage 2. Fold in stiffly whisked egg whites. Heat the butter in the omelette pan and cook as stage 4. It is difficult to cook through the thick soufflé mixture so when the bottom of the omelette is set place the pan under a moderately hot grill until just firm. Spread the hot chicken mixture over the omelette, fold and serve.

Spanish omelette: Heat chopped green or red pepper, peas, peeled onions etc. with the chicken in butter or oil at stage 1 then add to the beaten eggs at stage 2. Do not fold.

Chicken creams

you will need for 4–6 servings:

METRIC/IMPERIAL
1 teaspoon gelatine
300 ml/½ pint chicken stock
2 tablespoons dry sherry

225–275 g/8–10 oz cooked chicken breast
200 ml/⅓ pint double cream

1 Dissolve the gelatine in the highly-flavoured chicken stock and add the sherry.
2 Mince the chicken breast, blend with the stock and cool, but do not allow to stiffen.
3 Whip the double cream until it just holds its shape and fold into the chicken mixture. Spoon into 4–6 dishes and allow to stiffen.
4 Serve with toast and salad.

Variations:
Economy creams: Omit the sherry and double cream and blend the chicken and stock with white sauce (see page 41), using 25 g/1 oz butter, 25 g/1 oz flour and 200 ml/⅓ pint milk plus seasoning.

Asparagus creams: Substitute condensed asparagus soup for the white sauce or whipped cream or add chopped, well drained cooked or canned asparagus tips to either recipe (above).

Mousse of chicken: Flavour with chopped herbs or 1–2 teaspoons tomato purée at stage 2. Increase the amount of gelatine to 2 teaspoons. Fold in the whipped cream then 2 stiffly whisked egg whites at stage 3. Spoon into dishes and leave until set.

Mousse of chicken and ham: Use half chicken and half ham in mousse of chicken (above).

Chicken pancakes

There are a number of ways in which chicken can be used in a pancake mixture, and the following recipes show what delicious and economical dishes can be produced. The nourishing ingredients in the pancake batter and the sauces that fill them help to make a small amount of chicken go further. Try to serve as quickly as possible when filled, since the moist texture of the filling will spoil the pancakes if kept too long.

Pancake batter

you will need for 4–6 servings:
METRIC/IMPERIAL

100 g/4 oz plain flour	I egg
pinch salt	300 ml/½ pint milk

for frying:
fat or oil

1 Sift the flour and salt together. Add the egg and beat thoroughly.
2 Gradually add the milk, beating until smooth.
3 Heat just enough fat or oil to give a greasy layer at the bottom of a pan and pour in, using a spoon or jug, about 2 tablespoons of the pancake batter, or just enough to give a paper-thin layer in the pan.
4 Cook rapidly until brown on one side, then toss or turn and finish cooking on the other side.
5 Continue cooking the other pancakes, heating a little more fat or oil between pancakes if necessary.

Chicken pancakes

you will need for 4 servings:
METRIC/IMPERIAL

25 g/I oz butter or margarine	salt and pepper
2 teaspoons grated onion	pancake batter (see page 88)
225 g/8 oz cooked chicken	

for frying:
fat or oil

1 Heat the butter or margarine in a pan and fry the onion until soft.
2 Cut the cooked chicken into small pieces and mix thoroughly with the onion.
3 Season and add the mixture to the pancake batter.
4 Heat the fat or oil in a pan and pour in about 2 tablespoons of the pancake mixture.
5 Cook rapidly until brown on one side then toss or turn and finish cooking on the other side.
6 Serve the pancakes flat or roll them up and put on a hot dish. Serve at once with white, cheese or tomato sauce (see pages 41, 43).

Note:
To keep pancakes hot, put them on a hot dish and stand it over a pan of boiling water or in a low oven. Do not cover the pancakes.

Chicken pancakes gratinées

you will need for 4 servings:
METRIC/IMPERIAL

pancake batter (see page 88)	300 ml/½ pint white sauce (see page 41)
225–350 g/8–12 oz cooked chicken	50 g/2 oz grated cheese
	2 tablespoons cream

1 Cook the pancakes (see page 88); keep hot.
2 Chop or mince the cooked chicken.
3 Blend the chicken with half the sauce and keep hot.
4 Fill the pancakes with the chicken mixture, roll firmly and put on a hot flameproof dish.
5 Add cheese and cream to the remaining sauce and heat *gently* for a few minutes.
6 Coat the pancakes with the sauce and heat for a few minutes under a hot grill.

Chicken fritters

you will need for 4 servings:
METRIC/IMPERIAL
for the sauce:

25 g/I oz butter or margarine	150 ml/¼ pint milk or chicken stock
25 g/I oz flour	salt and pepper

for the filling:

350–450 g/12 oz–I lb cooked chicken	½–I tablespoon chopped chives
½–I tablespoon chopped parsley	2 tablespoons cream
	flour

for the batter:

50 g/2 oz flour	I egg
pinch salt	4 tablespoons milk

to fry:
deep fat

1 First make a thick white sauce (see page 41) with the butter or margarine, flour and milk or stock; add seasoning.
2 Mince or finely chop the chicken and add to the sauce with the parsley, chives and cream.
3 Allow to cool, form into round flat cakes and dust with a little flour.
4 Sift the flour and salt for the batter; add the beaten egg and milk. Beat until smooth then allow to stand.
5 Dip the cakes into the batter, lower into hot deep fat and fry until crisp and golden brown. Drain on absorbent paper and serve with vegetables or salad.

Variation:
A little cooked chopped asparagus, chopped ham, grated cheese or chopped tomato may be added to the filling.

Chicken soufflés

While cooked chicken lends itself to use in a soufflé mixture, it is possible to use raw chicken for a stronger flavour. Where possible use some chicken stock in the sauce.

The recipe for hot chicken soufflé produces a light firm texture. If you prefer the centre of a soufflé to be almost runny, use slightly more liquid. In the cold soufflés you must, of course, use cooked chicken.

If you make the hot soufflé mixture with egg whites only it will not be as likely to fall as when you use both yolks and whites; you can prepare the dish, cover it tightly and freeze for 3–4 weeks if wished. Allow to defrost at room temperature and bake at once. The cold soufflé can be frozen but tends to lose its delicate texture if stored for more than 2–3 weeks.

To steam chicken soufflés, put the mixture for a hot soufflé into the buttered soufflé dish, taking care to fill the dish to just over halfway. Put a piece of buttered paper lightly over the top of the dish then stand it in a steamer over a pan of boiling water and cook for the time given plus an extra 10 minutes.

until just tender. Add the stock and chicken to the roux at stage 2.

Variations:

Hot chicken and ham soufflé: Use 100 g/4 oz chicken and 100 g/4 oz ham.

Chicken soufflé surprise: Make 300 ml/½ pint white or other sauce (see pages 41, 42). Blend with 350 g/12 oz neatly sliced cooked chicken. Put into the bottom of a deep soufflé dish. Asparagus tips, sliced mushrooms etc. can be added. Cover with foil and heat for 10–15 minutes as at stage 6. Prepare the soufflé mixture as stages 2, 3 and 4 but omit the chicken and add 75–100 g/3–4 oz finely grated Cheddar, Gruyère or Parmesan cheese. Spoon over the hot chicken and bake as at stage 6.

Mushroom and chicken soufflé: Use only 100–150 g/4–5 oz chicken and add 50–75 g/2–3 oz finely chopped uncooked mushrooms at stage 3.

Spinach and chicken soufflé: Use sieved or liquidised spinach purée instead of the stock at stage 2.

Tomato and chicken soufflé: Use sieved fresh tomato purée instead of chicken stock at stage 2.

Hot chicken soufflé

you will need for 4 servings:

METRIC/IMPERIAL

225 g/8 oz cooked chicken	salt and pepper
25 g/1 oz butter or margarine	3 egg yolks
25 g/1 oz flour	2 tablespoons cream
150 ml/¼ pint chicken stock	4 egg whites

1 Put the chicken through a mincer twice to give a very fine texture.
2 Heat the butter or margarine in a pan, stir in the flour and cook for several minutes; gradually stir in the stock. Bring to the boil and cook until thickened and smooth.
3 Add the chicken, seasoning and egg yolks.
4 Mix well then fold in the cream and stiffly whisked egg whites.
5 Pour into a soufflé dish, filling just over three-quarters of the dish. If wished, put a band of paper round the outside, buttering it well where it stands above the dish.
6 Bake for approximately 30–35 minutes in the centre of a moderately hot oven (190°C, 375°F, Gas Mark 5).

Note:
A better and stronger flavour results if *raw* chicken is used. Use 300 ml/½ pint chicken stock. Simmer the finely minced chicken in the stock for 10–15 minutes

Cold chicken soufflé

you will need for 4–6 servings:

METRIC/IMPERIAL

225 g/8 oz cooked chicken breast	15 g/½ oz gelatine
3 eggs	2 tablespoons sherry or lemon juice
150 ml/¼ pint milk	salt and pepper
150 ml/¼ pint chicken stock	150 ml/¼ pint double cream

to garnish:

double cream	radishes

1 Prepare the soufflé dish: tie a double thickness of greaseproof paper round the dish to stand 7·5 cm/3 in above the top; grease the inside of the paper that stands above the dish with butter.
2 Mince the chicken very finely; separate the eggs.
3 Put the yolks into a basin with the milk and half the stock and whisk over hot but not boiling water until thick and creamy; add the chicken.
4 Dissolve the gelatine in the remaining stock (see page 14), blend with the egg mixture and add the sherry or lemon juice and seasoning. Cool and allow to stiffen slightly.
5 Whip the cream until it stands in peaks; whisk the egg whites and fold the cream then the egg whites into the mixture. Spoon into the soufflé dish.
6 Whip the remaining cream, season, and pipe over the top of the soufflé; garnish with tiny pieces of radish and remove the paper to serve.

Chicken in sandwiches

Chicken and turkey meat are excellent in all types of sandwiches. As the flesh is lean it is inclined to be dry, so be generous with the butter or use ingredients that will moisten the sandwiches.

Lean chicken is an ideal protein food for anyone on a diet. Top single slices of low-calorie bread or crispbread with any non-fattening topping or filling. If your diet is very strict, substitute large lettuce leaves for bread. Roll with a cocktail stick.

Freezing sandwiches

It may be convenient to prepare then freeze sandwiches. Avoid fillings with boiled or scrambled egg, crisp lettuce or other green salad vegetables, or generous amounts of mayonnaise. A *very little* mayonnaise, blended with other ingredients, should not be affected by freezing. Use within 1 month.

The following recipes are for closed sandwiches. Spread thin slices of bread with butter, butter with added ingredients or a savoury butter (see page 31). Spread one slice with the chicken filling then top with the second slice of buttered bread.

Chicken and lettuce: Chop the chicken, blend with a little mayonnaise and spread over crisp lettuce.

Chicken and almond: Blanch and chop almonds and blend with the butter; half cover the bread then top with thin slices of chicken and plain buttered bread.

Chicken and bacon: Use only a little butter on the bread and top with thinly sliced chicken then chopped cooked bacon rashers.

Chicken and celery: Chop the chicken fairly finely and cut crisp celery into tiny pieces. Blend with butter or mayonnaise and spread over plain or buttered bread.

Chicken and cheese: Blend minced or chopped chicken with cream cheese or grated or crumbled cheese moistened with a little seasoned cream or mayonnaise; spread over plain or buttered bread.

Chicken and cucumber: Peel cucumber and cut into wafer-thin slices; slice the chicken and blend with a little oil and vinegar dressing. Drain well; place on top of crisp lettuce on slices of buttered bread and top with more buttered bread.

Devilled chicken: Blend a pinch of curry powder, cayenne pepper and a few drops of Worcestershire sauce with butter, spread over bread then cover with sliced chicken.

Double-decker: Butter one slice of bread and cover with a chicken filling, top with another buttered slice then butter the other side and either repeat the filling or use a different chicken mixture, ham or bacon. Cover with a third slice of buttered bread.

Chicken and ham: Buttered bread can either be covered with very thin slices of ham and chicken, or the meat can be chopped fairly finely and mixed with butter or mayonnaise and flavoured with a little French or English mustard.

Harlequin chicken: Blend finely chopped red or green pepper, chopped (light and dark) chicken meat, chopped parsley and chopped celery or chicory with a little mayonnaise. Put on top of crisp lettuce on buttered bread and cover with more buttered bread. Cut into fingers and turn on their sides to serve so the colourful filling can be seen.

Chicken and gherkin: Blend chopped chicken meat and a few sliced or chopped gherkins with a little mayonnaise and spread on buttered bread.

Chicken and lemon: The delicate flavour of lemon adds interest to chicken sandwiches. Blend very finely grated rind of lemon and a few drops of lemon juice with butter and spread on bread, then add slices of chicken meat.

Chicken liver: Blend cooked and mashed or sieved chicken liver with mayonnaise, chopped parsley, a squeeze of lemon juice and chopped chives or spring onion. Spread on buttered bread.

Chicken and egg: Chop chicken meat and hard-boiled egg then mix with mayonnaise and seasoning and spread on buttered bread.

Chicken and peanut butter: Peanut butter blends well with chicken meat, particularly the dark flesh from the legs. Spread the bread generously with peanut butter, cover with thin slices of chicken, crisp lettuce and more bread spread with peanut butter.

Chicken and olive: Any olives (black, green, stuffed) are good in moderation in chicken sandwiches. Slice or chop the flesh of the olives and blend with the chicken meat and a little mayonnaise; put between slices of buttered bread.

Chicken and scrambled egg: Prepare chicken and scrambled egg mixture (see page 92) and cool. Add a little mayonnaise to moisten and spread on buttered bread. Top with lettuce and more buttered bread.

Soft-boiled egg: Soft-boil eggs, shell and chop. Blend with a little butter, seasoning and chopped chicken spread over plain or buttered bread.

Spiced chicken: Cover the buttered bread with thinly sliced chicken. Top with mayonnaise flavoured with grated nutmeg and grated horseradish, crisp lettuce and more buttered bread.

Chicken and tomato: Skin firm tomatoes, slice thinly and season well; place on a slice of buttered bread and cover with thin slices of chicken.

Chicken and watercress: Season sprigs of watercress well and chop then blend with butter. Spread over bread then cover with chicken meat and a second slice of watercress-buttered bread.

Open sandwiches

Scandinavian-type open sandwiches are ideal for serving chicken or turkey meat. Cut thin slices of white, brown, wholemeal or rye bread, spread generously with butter and add one of the toppings below. Serve with forks and knives or cut into small portions to eat with the fingers.

Avocado and chicken: First prepare French dressing (see page 80). Peel avocado pears, halve, cut the flesh into slices and marinate in the dressing for 5 minutes, then lift out. Arrange chicken slices on crisp lettuce and top with avocado slices and a little mayonnaise.

Cheese and chicken medley: Blend diced chicken with chopped nuts and diced cheese. Moisten with mayonnaise and spoon on to crisp lettuce. Garnish with piped cream cheese.

Chicken, bacon and prunes: Top lettuce with strips of chicken, crisp grilled bacon rashers and stoned prunes.

Curried chicken and banana: Dice cooked chicken and blend with sliced bananas and mayonnaise flavoured with a little curry powder. Spoon on to crisp lettuce and garnish with pineapple rings and gherkin fans.

Chicken and ham: Arrange sliced chicken and sliced ham, or rolls of ham filled with salad, on crisp lettuce. Top with mayonnaise flavoured with mustard.

Macedoine of chicken: Dice chicken neatly and blend with diced cooked potatoes, chopped celery and sweet corn. Bind with thick mayonnaise. Pile on to crisp lettuce and garnish with parsley and twists of lemon.

Chicken and orange: Top crisp lettuce with sliced chicken and well drained canned mandarin oranges. Garnish with cucumber slices.

Chicken Rossini: Top crisp lettuce with sliced chicken, pâté and crisp grilled bacon rashers.

Chicken and salads: Top crisp lettuce with sliced chicken, potato salad and Russian salad. Garnish with sliced tomato and/or gherkins.

Slimmers' sandwich: Spread low-calorie bread with a low-calorie spread. Top with crisp lettuce, sliced tomatoes, sliced cucumber and sliced chicken. Top with cottage cheese and twists of lemon.

Chicken and sweet corn: Top crisp lettuce with sliced chicken and sweet corn blended with chopped chives and mayonnaise.

Baked sandwiches

Make closed sandwiches with sliced chicken or one of the fillings or toppings in this section. Do not use lettuce, watercress or other crisp green salad ingredients.

Brush the outer sides of each slice of bread with melted butter. Place the sandwiches on a baking tray and put towards the top of a hot oven (220°C, 425°F, Gas Mark 7). It is important to preheat the oven. Leave for about 8–10 minutes (check after 5 minutes and reduce heat if browning too quickly) then serve hot.

Fried sandwiches

Make closed sandwiches without crisp green salad ingredients. For 4 sandwiches allow 1 egg and 2–3 tablespoons milk or chicken stock. Beat together, season lightly and pour on to a shallow dish.

Dip the sandwiches in the mixture, turn and coat on the other side. Do not leave for more than a few seconds in the egg mixture as the bread would become too soft.

Fry in hot shallow fat until golden on both sides. Serve at once. Crisp green salad makes a good accompaniment.

Serve it on toast

The following ideas are excellent for light evening or midday meals.

Club sandwiches

Allow 3 slices of toast per sandwich. Spread the first slice of hot buttered toast with one filing; top with a second slice of buttered toast and a second filling. Finally press the third slice of buttered toast on top and cut into 4 neat triangles. Garnish with salad and serve at once.

Note:
Sliced hot or cold chicken or one of the chicken mixtures could be one of the fillings, then have cooked ham, fried mushrooms, cooked bacon or fried, scrambled or sliced hard-boiled egg for the second layer.

Chicken rarebit

you will need for 4 servings:

METRIC/IMPERIAL

2–4 slices bread
50 g/2 oz butter or
 margarine
100–175 g/4–6 oz cooked
 chicken
100–175 g/4–6 oz
 Cheddar or other hard
 cooking cheese

15 g/½ oz flour
150 ml/¼ pint milk less
 1 tablespoon plus 1
 tablespoon beer or ale,
 or 150 ml/¼ pint milk
½–1 teaspoon made
 mustard
salt and pepper

to garnish:
chopped parsley

tomato slices

1 Toast the bread, spread with half the butter or margarine and keep hot; dice the chicken and grate the cheese.
2 Heat the remaining butter or margarine in a pan, stir in the flour, then add the milk and beer or ale. Bring to the boil and stir until thick and smooth; remove from the heat and add the chicken, cheese, mustard and seasoning but do not reheat the sauce. Meanwhile preheat the grill.
3 Spread the rarebit mixture over the hot toast, cook under the hot grill until just golden, garnish and serve.

Variations:

Celery chicken rarebit: Use the liquid from cooked or canned celery instead of the milk and beer at stage 2. Put well drained warmed celery hearts on the toast, then top with the rarebit mixture and grill.

Speedy chicken rarebit: Blend 25–50 g/1–2 oz butter and 1 egg or 2 tablespoons milk with 175–225 g/6–8 oz grated cheese, 100–175 g/4–6 oz diced cooked chicken and seasoning, plus a little Worcestershire sauce and/or beer to flavour. Spread on toast and grill.

Tomato chicken rarebit: Use tomato juice instead of the milk and beer at stage 2.

York chicken rarebit: Use only 50–75 g/2–3 oz cooked diced chicken and 50–75 g/2–3 oz cooked diced ham.

Chicken and egg toasts

you will need for 4 servings:

METRIC/IMPERIAL

4 small bacon rashers
100–175 g/4–6 oz cooked
 chicken
4 slices bread
25–50 g/1–2 oz butter or
 margarine

4 eggs
1–2 tablespoons milk or
 single cream
salt and pepper

to garnish:
sprigs of parsley

1 Make the bacon into neat rolls and grill until crisp and brown; dice the chicken.
2 Toast the bread, spread with butter and keep hot.
3 Heat the remaining butter or margarine in a pan.
4 Beat the eggs and add the milk or cream, seasoning and chicken.
5 Scramble the egg mixture in the hot butter or margarine until lightly set; pile on to the toast.
6 Top with bacon rolls and garnish with parsley.

Chicken scramble

you will need for 2–4 servings:

METRIC/IMPERIAL

100–175 g/4–6 oz cooked
 chicken
2–4 slices bread
50–75 g/2–3 oz butter or
 margarine

3 tablespoons milk or
 single cream
4 eggs
salt and pepper

to garnish:
sprigs of parsley

1 Cut the chicken into small pieces; toast the bread and spread with a little butter or margarine and keep hot.
2 Heat the remaining butter or margarine, add the milk or cream and the chicken and simmer gently for 2–3 minutes.
3 Beat the eggs lightly with a little seasoning then pour over the chicken mixture.
4 Stir gently until lightly set then spoon on to the hot toast and serve garnished with sprigs of parsley.

Variations:

Cheesy scramble: Add chopped chives to the eggs at stage 3 and 50–75 g/2–3 oz grated Cheddar or other hard cooking cheese just before the eggs are quite set at stage 4.

Chicken and corn scramble: Heat the chicken with about 100 g/4 oz cooked or canned well drained sweet corn in the milk mixture at stage 2.

Country scramble: Heat the chicken with about 175 g/6 oz cooked diced vegetables in the milk mixture at stage 2 or substitute 3 tablespoons of tomato juice or tomato purée for the milk.

Chicken and ham scramble: Use a mixture of diced chicken and lean ham at stage 2.

Chicken pipérade: Omit the milk. Skin and finely chop 2 tomatoes, 1 onion, 1 clove garlic and ½–1 green pepper (discarding core and seeds). Cook the vegetables in the hot butter or margarine until soft at stage 2 then add the chicken.

Index